Shaping Actors, Shaping Factors

in

Russia's Future

Publisher's Note

The books published in the *Forward Studies Series* contain a selection of research studies, reports, seminar or conference proceedings of the European Commission's Forward Studies Unit.

In publishing these works in the *Forward Studies Series,* the original material has undergone editorial rearrangement. Bibliographies have been added where necessary.

Forward Studies Series

SHAPING ACTORS, SHAPING FACTORS IN RUSSIA'S FUTURE

Foreword by Jérôme Vignon

St. Martin's Press
New York

Office for Official Publications
of the European Communities

SHAPING ACTORS, SHAPING FACTORS IN RUSSIA'S FUTURE

St. Martin's Press, Scholarly and Reference Division,
175 Fifth Avenue, New York, N.Y. 10010

First published in the United States of America in 1998

Printed in Great Britain

ISBN: 0-312-21603-3

Library of Congress Cataloging-in-Publication Data

Shaping actors, shaping factors in Russia's future / Forward Studies Unit
    at the European Commission.
        p.   cm.
    Includes bibliographical references (p.   ).
    ISBN 0-312-21603-3 (alk. paper)
    1. Russia (Federation)–Politics and government–1991– 2. Russia
(Federation)–Social conditions–1991– 3. Russia (Federation)-
-Forecasting. 4. Ukraine–Politics and government–1991–
5. Ukraine–Social conditions–1991– 6. Ukraine–Forecasting.
I. European Commission. Forward Studies Unit.
DK510.763.S465   1998
947.086–DC21   98–17418
                                                               CIP

Contents

Foreword

The publication *Shaping Actors, Shaping Factors in Russia's Future*
is the fruit of a project undertaken in 1994/95 to gain
understanding about the deeper socio-economic-political and
psychological structures governing the Russian transformation
process. Its original approach was 'to listen to the East', in order
to learn how Russians perceive the profound changes taking
place in their society, since it is often perceptions and
interpretations rather than mere facts that drive developments.
The study involved numerous Russian researchers producing
well over 1,200 pages and was updated in 1996 when a number
of Western experts also contributed.

This work was brought together by Paul Gerd Löser, an
economist, who served as adviser to the Forward Studies Unit
from 1990 to 1996. Using the initial material, supplemented by
various sources and many discussions with Russian and other
specialists and practitioners in the field, he produced this
synthesis.

The author chose to use an elaborated version of the
methodological approach used in an earlier study of the
Forward Studies Unit,[1] arriving at a holistic analysis by mapping
out all the actors and factors that are instrumental in Russia's
development and the way in which they are influencing it. The
result is a multi-layered analysis going beyond the customary
interpretation of day-to-day events, often concentrating on the
political establishment or the most visible features of the
Russian economy.

The study further develops a number of possible scenarios for
the future of Russia and presents their main features along with
the driving and braking forces behind them. The aim is to give

the reader a useful tool of analysis in order to understand the situation in Russia, and so be able to gauge for himself the possible direction in which the structural forces are leading the country against the background of current events. The choice of approach for the synthesis as well as the synthesis itself (concentrating on the underlying structural forces in the Russian society) makes this study viable as a self-standing piece of analysis for some time to come.

Jérôme Vignon
Director, Forward Studies Unit

Note

1 *The European Challenges post-1992 – Shaping Factors, Shaping Actors*, edited by Alexis Jacquemim and David Wright.

Acknowledgements

I would like to thank Anna Michalski for her help in revising the manuscript, Pamela Cranston and Eveline Hinterdorfer for their committed and efficient assistance, as well as Gilles Bertrand and René Leray for the many discussions.

However, sole responsibility for the contents of this publication remains with me. As with all publications of the Forward Studies Unit, it does not reflect European Commission's views nor those of its services.

Paul Gerd Löser
Adviser, Forward Studies Unit of the European Commission,
from 1990 to 1996.
Presently with the European Investment Bank

Introduction

In this book we look at where Russia is today, after six years of Gorbachevian *glasnost* and *perestroika*, and six years of Yeltsinite reforms and rule. Furthermore, we look at where Russia might go: towards democracy or authoritarianism? A market system integrating into the world economy or isolating itself? A nation state respectful of its neighbours or an empire again? A country occupied with internal reform or threatening to the outside world? Since there cannot be clear answers to these questions, a number of scenarios have been developed which may stimulate the reader's own thinking.

In the analysis of the present situation we have attempted to omit events and happenings that are without longer term significance. We have instead concentrated on the deeper social undercurrents and structural laws driving and directing these events. That is, we looked at the main *players*, whether they are more or less homogeneous social groups with broader common interests and narrower self-interest than was possible to define; or whether they are split and, therefore, represent less important or less predictable driving forces. We examined which social groups could develop similar interests and, therefore, might join forces and become major coalitions driving future developments. Probably the best example here is the interest of nearly all of the élite in the privileges and social status guaranteed by private property, rather than merit, as was the case up to now.

We then examined the main *factors* which might shape Russia's future such as the socio-psychological climate, its geopolitical situation and interests, and its economic potential and prospects. They constrain the behaviour and scope of action of the main shaping actors but, of course, they can be assessed only tentatively.

Finally, the interactions between the shaping actors and factors and the resultant tendencies for future developments were analysed. Whether these tendencies are valid and realistic was analysed by the use of *scenarios* (Chapter 2).

Thus, the analysis covers a large spectrum. Inevitably it has to, since without adopting a broad scope it would be difficult to understand the present situation and virtually impossible to build relevant scenarios.

This paper builds on the 1,200 page study *Shaping Factors, Shaping Actors in Russia* which was launched by the Forward Studies Unit of the European Commission in early 1994 and which had numerous contributions from Russian researchers. It was completed in May 1995 and continuously updated. It also profited from other literature and reports of journalists living in Russia, as well as from many discussions with Russian and Western experts.

Since the paper was originally intended for internal information purposes only, it does not refer to the different sources used. When the decision was taken to publish it, detailed identification of these sources proved an impossible task.

The scenario exercise and synthesis of the 'Shaping Actors, Shaping Factors' study have been carried out at different times. So there are repetitions for which we apologize. There may also be some contradictions, but Russia knows very many of these herself.

In Chapter 3, there is a 'Shaping Actors, Shaping Factors' exercise on Ukraine, since if Russia were to become an empire again, Ukraine would be the most difficult republic to reintegrate. And without Ukraine in the fold, it would not be possible to speak about a new Russian Empire.

Chapter 1

Shaping actors, shaping factors in Russia

1.1. THE MAIN PLAYERS AND THEIR SELF-INTERESTS

1.1.1. Who are the main political players?

Individual political personalities will continue to play an important role as catalysts or breakwaters for deeper social undercurrents. However, there is no point in speculating about the personalities, their vision or the face value of their propaganda since, in these unstable times, politicians and people behind the scenes rise and fall like comets and those managing to stay in power change their political views or character over time.[1] So we have tried to identify the main players and, whenever possible, their self-interests, on the assumption that their pursuit of them is a fairly accurate guide to future behaviour that might shape some future trends.

A strong power centre is characteristic of Russian political culture, as is the allocation of power to leading personalities rather than institutions. In this respect, history has repeated itself: the President and his apparatus are clearly at the centre of the political system (see Figure 1).

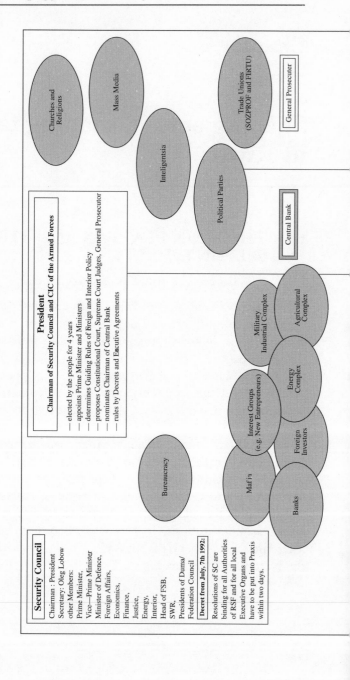

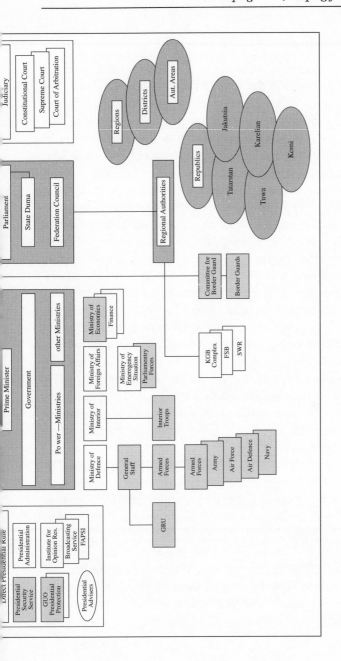

Figure 1 The Russian political system

The role and powers of the President

The government is more of an adjunct to the President than an independent power. All the main Ministries (i.e. Defence, the Interior, Foreign Affairs) are directly subordinated to the President, leaving few responsibilities for the government and even less scope for action, because it is the President who nominates the government and almost entirely controls the appointment of other executives.

The President has the right to rule by decree whenever there is a need to fill a legislative gap left by Parliament, and there are many, since in this period of economic and social transformation legislation runs far behind actual developments. Overturning presidential decrees requires a two-thirds majority in both the State Duma and the Federation Council which, under present circumstances, is nearly impossible to organize. The President can veto parliamentary legislation which, in order to be overturned, requires a two-thirds majority as well. He can ignore a parliamentary vote of no-confidence against the government, and in case Parliament confirms its vote within three months, the President can dissolve it – a scenario MPs will be keen to avoid for fear of losing their privileged position. The President is even entitled to proclaim a state of emergency and martial law, with his sole obligation to inform Parliament of this decision afterwards.

Overwhelming though the presidential power may be, it is all the more difficult to remove the President from office. The President can be dismissed by Parliament only if charges of state treason and serious crime are made against him by the Duma. The Supreme Court has to confirm the charge as an impeachable offence, and a two-thirds majority of the Duma is required to file it. In the case that it were to be successful, the same majority would be needed in the Federation Council in order to actually remove him from office. In fact, removing the President may even be more difficult, since it is he who nominates the members of the Constitutional Court, which also has to confirm the charges of state treason. This decision is subject to final approval by the Federation Council. In addition, the President and the State bureaucracy have many ways of putting pressure on the higher-ranking judges (i.e. by withdrawing privileges which are more important than salaries, etc.).

The judiciary

In short, the judiciary is still far from contributing to the checks and balance of Presidential power, a fact which it seems that the President and his apparatus have no interest in changing. They prefer to continue with the century-old tradition of considering law as an instrument of government and as a lever of power.

As to the role of the judiciary in general, a Council of Europe report of 1994 remarked that the rule of law had not yet been established: 'The concept that it should, in the first place, be for the judiciary to protect the individual has not yet become a reality in Russia.' For example, the penal code protects the state much more than the individual. The judiciary is not yet fully independent of the legislative and executive power; jurisdiction does not yet have clear priority over administrative decision-making. Analysing the Ministry of Justice's reform agenda reveals that essential parts of a rule of law are still lacking.

At the same time, it is true that some progress has been achieved. The power of the courts has been strengthened, and so has the position of the judges whose temporary contracts have been replaced by life-time appointments, enhancing the independence of their judgement. Also, judges are no longer nominated by administrative bodies but by the Russian President and to be eligible nowadays they have to give proof of much higher professional qualifications than previously.

Backlash against the judicial system

There have been backlashes. Notably, the power of the Constitutional Court, which had been increased by the adoption of the Constitution, was sized down immediately afterwards. Since June 1994, the Court is no longer entitled to examine, on its own initiatitive, the conformity of actions of high-ranking officials with the Constitution and the law. Such a move seems to indicate that those presently in power consider themselves as being above the law, not subject to it, just as has always been the case in Russian history. Such attitudes seriously hamper a more straightforward reform of the judiciary and its establishment as an independent power. The bureaucracy also has no interest in a strong judiciary, since it would compete with its own power.

The population at large never looked at the judiciary as a constitutional entity protecting them from the state, but as an instrument of state power and punishment. There is more disdain than respect for the judiciary, a tendency which has been reinforced by its inability to cope with the ever increasing criminality. As a consequence, people place higher hopes in a leader ruling with an 'iron fist' than in the establishment of a strong judiciary. It seems, therefore, that Russia still has a long way to go before a rule of law has become a reality. Its present absence is highlighted by a current saying in the Duma: 'Let's make one law which implements all the others.'

The presidential system and the governing institutions

Russia's constitutional reality could be described as an autocratic presidential system with a government as an adjunct, an 'emasculated' Parliament[2] as an annex, and an independent judiciary yet to be developed.

The presidential power builds on institutions which either are not explicitly provided for or exert an influence beyond what is foreseen by the Constitution: the *Presidential Administration,* the *Presidential Security Service* and the *Security Council.*

The *Presidential Administration* is regarded as the most important legislative and executive institution at the same time. It advises the President and prepares the torrent of decrees but it also interferes with their implementation by the federal government (and even the regional governments). It has developed into a large 'Byzantine' apparatus with about 4,500 highly-qualified staff members. There is very tough competition to join amongst the academic élite, which underlines where the power lies. It is not clear to whom the apparatus is accountable, whether it is, in fact, executing the will of the President, whether he himself, or someone else (the head of Staff, the President's personal assistant or the head of the Presidential Security Service), still clearly controls its activities. The Presidential Administration often bypasses both the government and Parliament, which makes it accountable to no one except (eventually) to the President. This is hardly conducive to the development of Russian democracy.

The *Presidential Security Service* seems to owe its strong role to its successive Chiefs'[3] closeness to the President. The Chief is in command of a force of 40,000 élite troops, for which, again, there is no legal basis. He seems to control all the security services of the country and to intervene in presidential legislation. Should Russia move towards a police state, as some fear, the role of this institution would clearly be further enhanced.

The *Security Council,* originally established as an advisory board, has developed into the primary decision-making body in the sphere of national security, for which, again, the Constitution provides no legal basis. It consists of the President, the Prime Minister, the Ministers for Internal and External Affairs, the Minister for Defence and the heads of both Chambers of Parliament, the directors of the 'KGB' complex (Federal Service for Counter-intelligence and Internal Intelligence

Service). The Security Council deliberates in secret, often without taking advice from the responsible ministries. Its resolutions are binding for all authorities of the Russian Federation and for all local executive organs. It seems to have decided exclusively on Chechnya and is now widely considered as the new Politburo.

Re-emergence of centralized power

So, following Gorbachev's attempts to open up the process of governance and to bring transparency into political decision-making, we see the old Tsarist and Soviet system re-emerge: an inner circle of personal advisers and unelected officials, many of them from the security services and the military, has again become the main source of policy and legislation. Power has once more become absolutely personalized. Personal access and emotional proximity to the President are the main sources of influence and political prestige (as such, they are decisive for a political career). The Yeltsin *kamarilla* stands to lose everything, especially the prestige and privileges connected with their office, if he were to be voted out of power. This fact sheds light on where their self-interest lies.

Some claim that the centralization and personalization of power makes the President appear to be more autocratic than he actually is. On major issues he would have to negotiate intensively with different élite groups. Therefore, the present system could better be described as an oligarchy. In fact, he has to negotiate with (democratically elected) regional leaders and some influential members of the military, but not with the other high-ranking officials who are nominated by him. Even Russia's new capitalists seem to depend on him to some extent, since there is no effective rule of law protecting them and their property. However, this dependence has become increasingly mutual as some of the new capitalists have developed into real business tycoons (partly with the Kremlin's benediction). They control important parts of the media and their massive support was essential for President Yeltsin's re-election in 1996.

Among all of the State institutions there is an ongoing struggle for control, which is reflected by the self-interest of politicians and bureaucrats in maintaining or increasing their power. The President is the only arbiter in such conflicts of interest, which tends to make responsibility and power shift further upwards (resulting in political paralysis when the President is unable to perform his duties). Such struggles are especially prevalent on the issue of assets and resources under privatization, or on the granting of privileges involving a monetary value (export licences, credits at preferential rates, etc.). In fact, the struggle over who distributes Russia's existing wealth (and to whom) seems to be the very source of much political in-fighting and is absorbing much of the energy of the political, bureaucratic and economic élite.[4] This state of affairs also means that no reform has been, nor will be, possible unless the (old) élite gets its share. They have used their capacity to block undesired initiatives, including political repression, since the fall of the Communist system; as the Russians say, 'the old *nomenklatura* has become the new one and has enriched itself'. Those who have been most successful in doing so now seem fiercely to block further reforms in order to preserve their social status.

Within the *nomenklatura*, the high and middle ranks of bureaucracy are invested with a great deal of power. According to a tradition that dates back to Tsarist times, it is they who interpret political instructions and legislation, not the judiciary. That is the main reason why Russians do not appeal to courts, which, in any case, they consider to be slow and unreliable. Rather, they prefer to settle conflicts by negotiation. It would not be in the bureaucracy's interest to change this situation, at least for the time being. Their interest lies more in legislation remaining unclear, vaguely implemented and opaque, and in the continuation of discretionary decision-making. This enhances their power and ensures the practice of back-scratching and flows of money from bribery, without which a decent standard of living would be unattainable.

Of course, behaviour is not only defined by self-interest and access to privileges, but also by maintaining traditions. For example, the bureaucracy in foreign policy, military adminis-trations and think-tanks was conditioned to view the West with suspicion, to say the least. Many, if not most of them, therefore, had strong reservations about Gorbachev's and Yeltsin's earlier positive orientation towards the West. They felt this to be unbalanced and out of line with Russia's geographic situation, geopolitical interests and perceived threats. The present re-orientation of foreign policy, which goes deeper than the nationalist rhetoric, therefore fits much better with the mind-set of the foreign and security policy bureaucratic élite. It is also the case, however, that some are very pro-Western and have been very critical of Russian policies, for example on Bosnia and Serbia.

1.1.2. What new role for the regions?

The regions of the Russian Federation (21 republics, 66 provinces plus Moscow and St Petersburg) act as a counter-balance to the concentration of power in the centre. They do have *de facto* local physical control and, therefore, can oppose, to some extent, centripetal tendencies.

The power of the regions

The immense size of the territory has always vested regional and local governors (and other élite including the military commanders) with enormous power since it was they who interpreted legislation and were finally responsible to the tsar (for whom the final results were more important than the methods used). Their opportunities to take liberties and enrich themselves were interrupted by Bolshevik controls and Stalinist terrorism, but in the Brezhnev years the old system of feudal dominions of sorts re-emerged. It was (loosely) kept together by the central Party apparatus, nominating the regional élite and deciding on their career advancement, and by the ministries of planning. When both of these cohesive forces disappeared, the regional élite successfully reached out for further power including legislative competence, resulting in a spontaneous regionalization of Russia.

The process was enhanced by the very weak centre existing between 1991 and 1993 when the Congress of People's Deputies and the Russian President fought for power, with both of them making promises and encouraging the regional leaders to 'take as many autonomous rights as you want' in order to pull the leaders into their camp. Spontaneous regionalization reached its culmination in autumn 1993, and the siege of the White House and dissolution of the Congress of People's Deputies (which in some ways represented the regions, as the election to the Congress strongly favoured regional/local bosses) marked the end of the regionalization tendency for the time being.

Change in balance of power

The new Constitution (adopted in December 1993) significantly cut back the regions' enlargement of control. The Chechnya war was another strong warning signal sent by the centre to the centrifugal forces in the regions, especially to ethnically motivated struggles for independence, that it will not tolerate a disintegration of the Russian Federation.

However, the distribution of power between the centre and the regions is not clear. Are regional bosses and businessmen to profit from the rich resources of Siberia regardless of the interests of the country as a whole? How far should the regions be permitted to set up their own fiscal systems independently of

Moscow? How much should they contribute to the federal budget and how much should the poorer regions be allowed to get from it?

The Constitution does not provide clear answers to these questions. Instead, there are many individual arrangements which create dynamics of their own towards continued negotiations for the most favourable treatment. Attempts by the central government to impose its policies by nominating regional governors subordinated directly to the President have not added much to make relations between Moscow and the regions clearer. It is not clear whether the governors are, in practice, on top of, below or parallel to the elected governments of the regions and, hence, to what extent they can exert influence.

In other words, the balance of power between the centre and the regions is not yet settled in a satisfactory way. It cannot be settled as long as it remains unclear in what direction Russia will move: a democratic Russia might decide in favour of a *real* federalization with clear constitutional provision as to the rights and responsibilities of the regions; an authoritarian Russia would try to cut back further on their powers and establish new vertical command structures.

Meanwhile, one should assume that the regional élite will have an interest in strictly opposing anything which could lead to a strengthening of the centre, depriving them of much of the autonomous rights they have acquired in recent years. Notably, one might expect them to oppose an adventurous foreign and security policy because this could result in a re-militarization of the country and consequently a re-centralization. Thus, the regional élite could be regarded as political stabilizers on some issues. On the other hand, the more rural and backward regions also represent a burden for the development of democracy since many of them are governed like personal fiefdoms, which is not conducive to the spreading of democratic values. The regional élites' immediate self-interest seems to favour muddling-through policies in Moscow, providing them with ample opportunities to further extend their *de facto* power as they did (again) successfully during President Yeltsin's illness and the resulting paralysis of the centre.

1.1.3. Will the military and the enforcement agencies remain politically neutral?

The role of the military would decline if democratization continued; on the other hand, it would increase if authoritarian rule were to re-emerge (or if Russia's security interests were to be threatened). With Russia's political system being somewhere in between democracy and authoritarianism, the military and the secret services' loyalty is of vital importance for the political leadership, and they are therefore potential players whose interests will need to be taken into account by any President.

Role and power of the military

It is true that Russia has no tradition of the military being a player on its own, reaching for political power. However, it could not be considered as a blindly obedient instrument in the hands of political power either. The Soviet leaders were always aware of the risks of the military's switching loyalty and lending support to competing factions in the Party hierarchy or of a 'Bonaparte' *putsching* himself into power, and they therefore tied the military and KGB leaders closely into the Party structures.

Tying the armed forces[5] closer to the Presidential regime and establishing counter-forces within it in order, eventually, to neutralize their less reliable elements is another tendency that can be observed today. The *coup d'état* attempt carried out by reactionary Communist forces against Gorbachev in August 1991 and the initial reluctance of the military to take part in

15

Yeltsin's *coup d'état* (as some call it) in October 1993[6] have accelerated efforts to make the army more reliable.

To whom does the military owe allegiance?

The 'new military doctrine' adopted immediately after the events of October 1993 (by the Security Council, in the face of parliamentary opposition) subordinates all of the armed forces directly to the President and legalizes their possible use in internal conflicts. They can now be called upon to intervene in the event of an attempt to forcibly topple the constitutional system or to undermine the organs of government and state power. This provision is rather ambiguous since the question of to whom the military owes loyalty, to the Constitution or the President, was not answered clearly (relevant in the case of a *coup d'état* from the top). The doctrine further allows for the use of the armed forces in cases where the territorial integrity or other vital interests of Russia are endangered (which provide the legal cover for the intervention in Chechnya). It also can be used to fight organized crime, terrorism and the dealings of 'other organizations' aimed at destabilizing the internal situation.

Thus, the President *legally* has at his disposal a powerful instrument for all sorts of internal policing purposes, just as was the case during the Communist regime. However, many of the officers are highly critical of these provisions in the military doctrine (which reportedly was adopted in spite of the opposition of the Ministry of Defence), and quite a number of generals who were not consulted about the Chechnya operation, in fact, refused to participate in the war. Furthermore, the fact that many young Russian conscripts surrendered or deserted rather than fight against civilians at home seems to suggest that the President cannot fully rely on the Russian Army when faced with internal conflicts.

Winning the Army's loyalty

There are, therefore, clear attempts to create a loyal army within the Russian Army, closely tied to Yeltsin's political fate. The closer the higher-ranking officers are to the President, the more privileges and budget allocations they seem to be granted, and the more their views are heard. However, it is not guaranteed that the policy of establishing close personal ties will pay off in terms of the entire Russian Army being loyal to the President in the event of internal political power struggle. With the spread of democratic values, many officers have come to consider the non-involvement of the army in internal politics as essential, because if they were to become party to a conflict there would be a risk of a splitting of the army and it could be used as cannon fodder in political in-fighting. The fear of a split stems from the fact that the officer corps is politically fragmented with orientations ranging from reform-minded democrats to ultra-nationalists hostile to the reforms. Only a minority of the higher ranks, according to unofficial sources, is loyal to the Communists.

The Army factions

The Russian Army is further divided, especially at the level of the Ministry of Defence and the General Staff, which is split into the 'career military group' (the 'aristocracy') and the 'Afghanistan group' (the 'parvenus') along with other groups. While all the groups at the senior echelons of the Ministry of Defence seem to be 'politically moderate', they differ in their orientations towards the West. The 'aristocracy' is more traditionalist, conservative and anti-Western, while the 'parvenus' consist mostly of relatively young officers closely linked by personal ties. The latter group still seems to dominate the Ministry and is not fundamentally opposed to cooperation with the US, NATO and other Western institutions (former

Minister Grachev was an active proponent of 'Partnership for Peace'). However, the military 'aristocracy' seem to have strong allies among the regional and local commanders who are also very critical of the Ministry's pro-Western attitude. It is not known what is more important to them, the Ministry's general policy orientations or their personal regional or local power and responsibility for their troops, which seems to lead to quite a number of them lending their strong arm to the respective regional/local political leaders (including instructions to their soldiers for whom to vote). Depending on future develop- ments, they could become a force for oppressive stability in their regions ('Peace Lords') or mavericks ('War Lords'). There are also strong suspicions that the top ranks of the armed forces are highly corrupt, selling weapons and misusing budget funds. They, after all, also want their part of the cake in the privatization of Russia.

Thus, the Russian Army is all but monolithic. The only common feeling held amongst its officer corps seems to be strong discontent resulting from their general and severe loss of social status (reinforced by the army's humiliation in Chechnya) and from their very poor material conditions (severe budgetary cutbacks, inadequate housing for the officer corps, 75 per cent of the officers living below the poverty level).

Whether the President could rely more on the other sections of the armed forces is not clear. However, their importance and influence in decision-making (within the Security Council) seem to have increased over the last three years, at the expense of the Ministry of Defence. This may reveal perceptions held by the President of them being more reliable, but it also clearly reflects the fact that these forces, notably the Interior Troops and the Border Guards, are experienced combat units deployed in most of the ethnic conflict and hot-spot areas of which there is no shortage in the Russian Federation and the post-Soviet space as a whole (according to Russian analysts there are some 150 'potential Chechnyas').

The 'KGB' faction

Finally, the President controls the large former 'KGB' complex with its own élite troops. It is not subordinated to any noteworthy parliamentary and judiciary control and, thus, it is an instrument of power which remains a standing temptation even to a democratic president. However, whether the agents and troops of these services would actually follow the instructions of the President is not clear. The KGB was one of the original supporters of *glasnost* and *perestroika*. It was the best informed about economic and technological developments abroad, and about Russia's growing backwardness. The former head of the KGB and the party's General Secretary, Yuri Andropov, brought Gorbachev into power and, therefore, one might assume that quite a number of KGB people are reform-minded. In addition, they are well trained, with some 80 per cent of them having an academic background, which offers them ample opportunities to start a business career as many of their old colleagues have done. This may make the KGB people less dependent and, therefore, reluctant to serve obediently a Communist President, for example.

So, despite the efforts to tie the armed forces and enforcement agencies into the Presidential regime, questions as to their loyalty remain open. Yet, even though more generals actively participate in political life, including the Duma, than in any other 'democratic' country, the internal divisions in the army seem to oppose the emergence of a 'Bonaparte', even more so as he could not offer any convincing solutions to Russia's many and complex problems. However, the President, in order to win over their loyalty, would have to respect their broader interests and self-interest. The broader interests of the military lies in Russia playing a leading role in the post-Soviet space and is capable of defending its geopolitical interests between 'two continents and three oceans'. Were this more activist orientation to be confirmed, this would imply not only the modernization of the army and its equipment, but also an improvement of the army's social status contributing to enhance the officer corps' self-esteem. To play an important and respected role is where the army's self-interest lies.

1.1.4. Who are the economic players?

The new economic élite and the dynamic part of the old one are clearly the most important, and, at the same time, the most predictable of the driving forces. Parts of the new business class are extremely young and active, but whether they are willing to take commercial risks and build new factories still remains to be seen. For the time being, they concentrate on service industries which do not need start-up capital as much as 'good relations' and, in addition, offer the highest profits. Fortunes are made by buying raw materials and commodities at rouble prices and selling them for dollars on the world market, by activities in commodities and stock exchanges, as well as in the banking and media business. Industrial business, however, is rather neglected except for the building industry. Logic would suggest that both new and old economic élite have an interest which is firstly to further extend their hold on existing assets, resources and economic 'rents',[7] and only then to concentrate on restructuring and expanding business, unless of course it is new business. In other words, Russian capitalists are not in a hurry to modernize industry as long as there are other opportunities for making profits.

Getting hold of assets is easier if unclear legislation continues. Only when a significant majority of the new owners feel satisfied with what they have got (in the redistribution process) will they develop an interest in having their property legalized and protected by a rule of law. Meanwhile, good relations with politicians, bureaucrats and the Mafia (protecting their property) serve this purpose.

Economic groups' political influence

It seems that the new and old economic groups alike exert an increasing influence on presidential and parliamentary legislation. They certainly differ as to the desired speed of further reforms, the degree of market deregulation and economic competition. However, none of these groups seems to be interested for the time being in free competition, including open borders. Russian tradition is to negotiate and find arrangements rather than to openly compete and, in addition, all of them feel too weak to cope with international competition. Even more importantly, there are no competitive structures, but thousands of monopolies, whose dismantling meets strong resistance from both the directors and the workers who have together become the new owners as a result of privatization.

Corporate and interventionist policies

Therefore, the trend clearly is towards corporatist and interventionist economic policies guaranteeing monopolistic rents and protection from foreign competition in almost all of the important economic sectors:

- The *military industrial complex (MIC)* favours slow reform since the conversion to civil production is a painful process and requires capital and know-how that it does not have. Moreover, conversion is something which is hardly feasible in cases where the production consists only of sophisticated weapons. Therefore there are no consistent and effective conversion policies but many hopes of entering the world market of high-tech products (aerospace etc.). The MIC is protectionist as to the civil products it produces; on the other hand, it is pushing hard for the export of weapons to any interested country, and has been very successful in doing so

21

over the last three years. According to the MIC officials, this is the only way of raising the money they need to restructure and modernize their factories. Finally, it goes without saying that the MIC is pushing hard for the modernization of military equipment and for research on sophisticated weaponry to continue in order to preserve its technological know-how. The MIC is also the most zealous supporter of the economic reintegration of the CIS, since its factories are distributed all over the area with only the final assembly lines being located in Russia. Reintegration would bring back its sub-contractors and, hence, strengthen its economic potential.

- The *agricultural complex* is opposed to fundamental reforms including private land-ownership, and is outrightly protectionist. It may even rely on the support of peasants or agricultural workers who hang on to age-old local traditions, collectivism, egalitarianism and suspicion towards private property to achieve its objectives. The bosses of the agricultural complex would clearly like this support to become permanent, thereby enhancing their personal power.

- The *energy complex* is keen on the privatization of monopolistic rents and on exporting, and especially on hard currency earnings which provide it with the financial power to modernize its production and infrastructure and to buy up industrial companies in Russia as well as in other republics. It is keen on acquiring foreign technology but its interest in sizeable foreign participation in the exploitation of energy resources is declining. It is more interested in getting access to Western capital markets, which would provide it with the money needed to buy foreign technology and extend its economic power. Access to foreign capital markets would also allow the energy complex to bypass the banking and financial sector with which it competes for economic and political power.

- The *new entrepreneurs'* interests differ according to their sector of activity, but they are certainly among those who have a strong interest in continued economic reform. The financial sector has indeed already demonstrated protectionist instincts since it would suffer by open competition with renowned and trustworthy Western financial institutions. With competition between Russian banks becoming increasingly stronger and with a banking crisis looming, it is quite possible that they will become even more protective. The *trade sector* as a whole is certainly interested in open borders with the CIS as well as with others, but the traders with the best connections with the bureaucracy might favour a controlled trade with trade privileges for only a few.

Both sectors have accumulated considerable amounts of capital in recent years which are used to acquire industrial companies (i.e. by giving credit to the government in exchange for its share holdings in industry; and eventually by buying out workers' shares). The first large *financial industrial groups* have already emerged and they could become the most important driving force for the modernization of management and industry.[8]

- *Foreign investors*, of which there are not that many, are encouraged to start businesses, but there seems to be a tendency developing to drive them away once the new business has begun to flourish. In addition, foreign investors are no more free-trade-minded than the Russians since business in a protected market can prove to be much more lucrative. Some of them now seem to secretly buy into Russian companies in order to prepare for a protectionist Russia. They do not care about eventual reciprocal Western trade barriers because they want to benefit from the huge Russian market and not to produce for export (except in the energy sector) which they could do from more convenient locations.

23

1.1.5.   Organized crime

The power struggle over the distribution of assets and resources has mobilized enormous energy, including criminal energy. Russia has known Mafias since the Brezhnev era, and many of them seem to have emerged from close personal ties between criminals in the many Gulag Archipelagos. The Mafia were the only functioning organization when the Soviet state structures were dismantled. The subsequent weakness of state power, i.e. the absence of a rule of law, has allowed criminal organizations to penetrate most of the Russian economy. The bureaucracy, judiciary, police, militia, security services and even politicians are paid low salaries and, in addition, their jobs are insecure, which makes them interested in using their positions for illegal lucrative business dealings or in protecting their positions. Thus, criminal and financially powerful organizations seem to have an easy play in getting hold of export licences for raw materials, gold or diamonds and have not too much to fear when engaging in drugs and arms trafficking.

Mafiosa power

It is said that mafiosi control up to 80 per cent of Russia's trade sector and 40 per cent of the economy as a whole. Also large parts of the new commercial banks are said to be in the hands of the Mafia. They seem to be keen on setting up branches in the West, obviously in order better to organize capital flight and to participate in international money-laundering. As there is no rule of law, many other business people depend to some extent on the Mafia's protection services; nearly all seem to pay for them, although the price is high (reportedly 10 to 20 per cent of profits). Those who do not, have to invest in their own protection service (in some banks, bodyguards etc. account for a quarter of the staff).

Although the Mafia is not a homogeneous group, but

consists of some 20,000 gangs (according to Yeltsin), their commonly shared interest is clearly to delay the emergence of a rule of law. One may argue that the Mafia, too, will sooner or later want to turn to serious legal business and develop an interest in a rule of law that protects them. However, this may take a long time, as many examples in different parts of the world show. Presently, efforts to fight the Mafia seem to be a lost battle since it is much better equipped than the police forces which, in addition, are very corrupt. Therefore, many believe that domesticating the Mafia will be possible only by the use of brutal authoritarian force which, however, would delay further the emergence of a rule of law.

Meanwhile, the Mafia is weakening the country by extracting money from the economy and investing it in highly liquid assets only, or directly in foreign assets, by paralysing economic legislation and its proper implementation and by frightening off honest people and foreign investors from entering business.

Popular attitudes to crime

The population is as fearful of the Mafia as it was of the former KGB, and shocked by the huge increase in crime. Not all of it can be attributed to the Mafia, of course. With 70 per cent of the population currently living at or below the official poverty line, theft and robbery (often ending up in murder) have become a question of survival for many. Their level of inhibition is low, as their favoured victims, i.e. the (rich) 'new Russians', are considered to be thieves and robbers (namely of state property). Still, the population at large associates all sorts of crime (as well as all sorts of businesses charging higher prices than in Soviet times) with the Mafia.

Fighting the Mafia and in particular establishing law and order is, therefore, the most popular public concern, even if it results in 'strong rule'. Many seem to believe that the

Communists, if no one else, would do this successfully (although historically, the emergence of the Mafia can clearly be traced back to the Brezhnev era).

Since many of its groups are organized along ethnic lines, the Mafia is also playing into the hands of ultra-nationalists.[9] This may well further intolerant attitudes and, therefore, the use of violence against ethnic groups.

1.1.6. The Russian Orthodox Church

The Church has a double role, religious and socio-political.

The new spirituality

Joining the Church in recent years has been a fashionable trend, but the 'new spirituality' seems to be rather shallow. Russian Orthodoxy has not yet developed any form of social teaching which might extend its function into the day-to-day lives of ordinary people. Its teaching is fundamentally mystical and sacramental and, therefore, inclined towards a puritanical and anti-worldly attitude. It offers neither consolation nor satisfactory moral guidelines in this time of profound change and does not seem to contribute much to the new orientation of the Russian mind.

In addition, a deep sense of suspicion lingers from the days when the KGB had infiltrated the whole Church structure. Stalin's persecution of all religions, which, according to some figures, led to the execution of 200,000 priests, has left in place today an establishment that is not only mistrusted, but also of mediocre ability. Furthermore, the indoctrination that the people suffered under the former Communist regime, and its insistence upon blind faith in the Soviet myth, has left deep wounds in the Russian psyche: in some way, the sudden and total disappearance of the Communist myth has now made people reluctant to believe in 'believing'. Although the proportion of people who consider themselves to be believers grew rapidly after liberalization in 1990, it has levelled out after 1993 at 40 per cent (a widely confirmed result). The proportion of true believers may, however, be much smaller still, not more than 5 per cent, some say. The great majority of the population, therefore, is still agnostic or atheist, and there is a great reluctance on the part of the new generation of Russians to embrace Orthodoxy.

The Church and politics

More important here is the socio-polititical role of Russian Orthodoxy. The Church, along with the army, remains a pillar of Russian society and its moral authority is held in rather high esteem, even among the 'non-believers'. A *Declaration of Cooperation* between these two pillars was signed in 1994 announcing 'the re-establishment of a thousand-year tradition which binds the army and the church'; this suggested the emergence of a bilateral pact adding immense strength to the 'power arm' of the state.

However, the Church is not monolithic, but split into different groups and these internal divisions are instrumental in undermining its effectiveness. There are those who adhere to an independent Church, others who argue for a State Church, those who take an ecumenical stance and, finally, the fundamentalists. Who holds the balance of power amongst these groups is not exactly known. The ultra-conservative wing is extremely politicized and increasingly dominating public discussion. It seems to be moving in the direction of chauvinism and, therefore, could become a dangerous propaganda tool for intolerant attitudes and the rebuilding of the Russian Empire.

Such attitudes could be reinforced by attempts of non-Russian Patriarchs to separate from the Patriarchate of Moscow. The attempted schism of the Estonian Orthodox

Church immediately raised fears about the Patriarchate of Kiev eventually following and was, therefore, met by strong opposition. The Patriarchate of Moscow obviously wants to retain its supreme position and spiritual leadership in the post-Soviet space. Therefore, it seems to be the 'spiritual' ally of all political leaders pleading for deeper integration of the CIS (though not necessarily for its full domination by Russia) to ward off risks of schism.

Intolerant attitudes, furthermore, cause many Westerners to express concern about the impact on the Muslim populations along and beyond Russia's southern flank. For the moment Islam and Russian Orthodoxy seem able to co-exist. The reason is the many pronounced varieties of local nationalism alive in these regions which will counteract all-encompassing Islamic brotherhood, and keep the Muslim populations fragmented. However, Russians would not discount the possibility of conflict in the future. Nationalism combining religious extremism with divisions along ethnic lines, Yugoslavia-style, is a potential scenario.

1.1.7. The emergence of democratic features

There has been a proliferation of political parties (see Figure 2) which are not, however, parties in the Western sense, but rather autocratic, personalized election clubs in which material self-interest and access to privileges often seem to be more important than political motivation.

They have no clear profile, if indeed any, and only form coalitions depending on the issue in question. This contributes to a lack of transparency and hardly allows the population to identify with parties. There is a growing influence of economic pressure groups or individual business tycoons, and Mafia ties also seem important for financing election campaigns. Some even start to worry about criminals and local puppets being elected to the State Duma.

The political parties lack effective organization at the national as well as the local levels; and, most importantly, have not established a link between the preferences of society and the political orientations of the government, i.e. there is no such thing as 'the party(ies) in power' (since the power is with the President).

Across the political spectrum

The only party which presently could claim to perform such functions and which effectively could build on a strong organization is the Communist Party (if a Communist President were voted into power). The right of the political spectrum is fragmented and poorly organized. There is no real 'political centre', moderately liberal and reform-minded, which could act as a political stabilizer.[10] At the very right end of the spectrum there are Zhirinovsky's 'Liberal Democrats' and a slowly but constantly growing number of national-patriotic or outright chauvinistic parties, glorifying 'Great Russia' (often identical with the USSR). They not only grow in numbers but also in size.

At the extreme ends of the political spectrum, therefore, there are strong parties, whereas the middle can be characterized as a 'black hole'. Still, some 40 per cent of the population vote for the parties in the middle. However, this should in no way be interpreted as 40 per cent voting for democracy and market economy. Some may, but the majority of those voting for a party in the middle seem to do so because they are disgusted by the extremists on the left and the right. Such voting behaviour seems to suggest that there is no positive and stable commitment to the parties in the middle of the spectrum. Therefore, one might say that despite the growth in number of parties a real multi-party system is still non-existent in Russia.

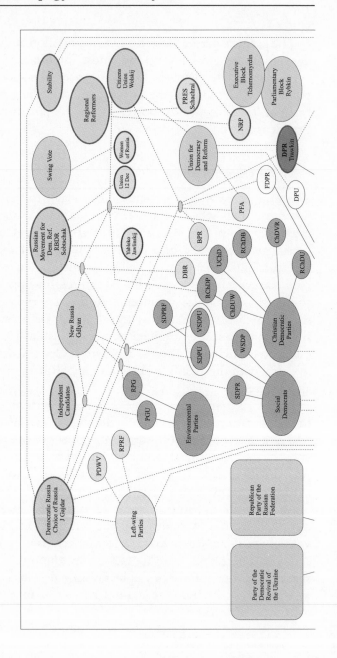

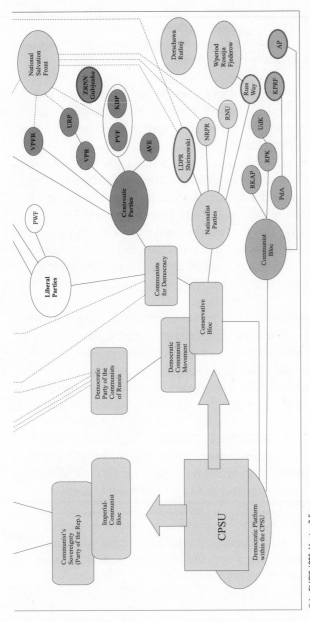

© by EUCIS 1995, Version 2.5

Figure 2 The political parties

Lack of multi-party system

There are strong braking forces working against the establishment of a stable multi-party system:

- Russian society (still) lacks a large middle class, or rather, bourgeoisie, with a strong interest in continued reform, improvement of its status and opposed to new political experiments and extremism.
- The Presidential system with the limited role of Parliament may not be conducive to the emergence of strong democratic parties. Even if the democratic camp could overcome its fragmentation, it would still not represent a majority in the present Duma. The President would always have to overrule the Duma's legislation through vetoes and decrees, thereby discrediting the democrats and the Duma in general, a development which, in the end, would benefit the extremists.
- Growing regionalism hampers the emergence of new nation-wide parties, and especially in a political climate in which people are alienated and apathetic about politics or more interested in parochial bread-and-butter issues.
- More fundamentally, political organizations that fight amongst themselves for power but are nonetheless not enemies and which can build coalitions with each other, contradict Russian political culture. There never existed a liberal culture of controversy and a search for balance and compromise between differing positions. Instead, differing points of views were (and are) considered solely as temporary ones which have to be overcome resulting in either consensus or a split.[11] Therefore, political parties are perceived by most people as an expression of destroyed harmony, bad feelings and fractionalism, lack of consensus and, therefore, of political weakness.
- Such perceptions kept President Yeltsin from stepping to the

top of a party. Instead, he preferred to pretend staying 'above politics', not representing particular 'party' interests, but the interests of the people. Obviously, such emphasis on the non-partisan character of political power is not only hampering the emergence of strong democratic parties, it is also discrediting the existing democratic groups and the Duma as well. In fact, the Parliament's status has greatly suffered and anti-parliamentarianism is on the increase.

So (Western) hopes for an early emergence of a multi-party system (and a Western-type democracy) are proving too optimistic. Russian political culture, i.e. the utopia of a general, social and political consensus in combination with an unchallenged leadership (voicing such consensus), is working against it and will not change in the near future.

1.1.8. Weak civil society

There has also been growth in the number of trade unions which, however, have not yet established themselves as political and social players.

The trade unions

The old unions, though having added 'independent' to their names, are not yet emancipated from their former role, which was to act as transmission belts for the Party and managers' power interests rather than real supporters of workers' interests. Russian workers do not trust them but they do not resign their membership (which in Soviet times was a must) for fear of this being interpreted as socially unacceptable or a challenge to 'the powers that be'. They do not expect much from their unions, as caring for social problems is perceived as being the State's responsibility, and, because of that, most people seem to be satisfied with the social services (holiday vouchers, nursery schools and crèches or firewood, for example) that the old unions still provide.

As for the new unions, which have emerged along with the new democratic orientations, their membership remains low and is still decreasing. Yet their influence is important in some industries, such as mining. Joining them is tantamount to revolt and reluctance to do so increases in indirect relation to the distance of the industry or plant from Moscow or St Petersburg, as does the reluctance to vote for democratic parties.

So the trade unions, though strong in numbers and membership, are still effectively rather weak, a fact which is best illustrated by wages remaining unpaid for months, (resulting, together with Russian inflation rates, in a very high [downward] wage-flexibility spiral). The very low (official) unemployment rate can hardly serve as proof to the contrary. Rather, this seems to result from subsidies to industry, pressure from all sorts of authorities on managers to cut down the workforce prudently and, eventually, pressure by the workers who have become co-owners of companies on their managers. Whether the workers' co-ownership will hamper the emergence of economically and socially stronger trade unions is an open question. However, this seems to be a condition for the unions to become more attractive to their members, to contribute to thinking in terms of self-help (thus overcoming the prevailing social infantilism of expecting everything from an omnipotent ruler) and, thus, to establish themselves as political players, eventually forging close links with reform-minded political parties.

The business associations

There is a continuously growing number of business associations organizing the more than eleven million entrepreneurs and self-employed, managers of larger companies and banks as well as owners of small shops. They share a common interest which is to get rid of the bureaucracy's stranglehold of the economy but are, in fact, rather disunited.

The 'New Russian' businessmen

The 'red directors' (old/new company directors), *de facto* owners before, *legal* (co-) owners now with their well-established old boys' network with the bureaucracy have interests which are dissimilar to those of the self-made 'New Russian' businessmen. In addition, most of them distrust each other or would like to obtain tailor-made privileges and, therefore, prefer to establish individual relations with the bureaucrats which, of course, strengthens the latter's position. And even where the business community managers somehow agree on a proposal to reform the decision-making of economic policies or on a specific issue, the bureaucrats seem to be quite well organized to answer quickly with counter-proposals of the government, leaving their responsibilities and power untouched. Thus, a fragmented business community is facing a bureaucracy which is rather united when it comes to defending the prospect of developing into a wealthy bourgeoisie thanks to a continuous flow of bribe money. One might expect this imbalance to continue unless very tough decisions are taken at the top political level or until a rule of law has become a reality and protects the individual from the state and bureaucracy.

Other organizations

As to other organizations of a civil society, not very many exist. The numerous environmental groups which had successfully opposed the adventurous deviation of Siberian rivers but could not stop the daily reckless destruction of the environment, have been weakened considerably. Many of them merely served as camouflage for political opposition groups which, since *glasnost*, are no longer needed. More importantly, the Russian people are presently almost entirely concerned with their economic survival and, thus, pay little attention to the environment. Therefore, there is no social nor political pressure to address the very severe problems of environmental pollution and their health-threatening consequences. Neither do the Russian people have the time and interest to build up and engage in other institutions of a civil society. *The Mothers of Russian Soldiers* seems at present to be the only broadly based civil movement. It opposed the Chechnya war and strongly supported the President's election promise to abolish the universal compulsory military service.

1.1.9. Media dominated by the government and the new capitalists

The media have been vigorous supporters of reforms and they remain the strongest critics of the current state of affairs. However, much has changed since the early 1990s. With the increasing consolidation of presidential power, the President's previously favourable attitude towards a free media gave way to attempts to control it. Already in December 1992, a 'Federal Russian Information Centre' was created, which tried to bring the media under presidential control. Political pressure on journalists increased strongly with the start of the Chechnya war in December 1994. Yet, the attempts to impose conformity have not been completely successful, mostly due to the large number of courageous journalists fighting for free media even under the most difficult conditions. However, the free press has lost much of its influence as a result of the economic crisis. The liberalization of prices (1991–93) made paper prices explode and newspapers unaffordable for most people, especially those living outside big cities. Many of the newly founded newspapers disappeared from the market and those which survived saw their circulation dwindle to one tenth of the 1991 figure.

People in the provinces now depend on regional and local newspapers which have proliferated as a result of Russia's regionalization. However, these papers mostly depend on financial support of regional and local authorities and are subject to much more vigorous political control. Their quality, especially with regard to critical political reporting, is poor. For the provincial press, the Chechnya war hardly took place, for example.

Besides political pressure on journalists, they also experience pressures on behalf of criminal organizations. A Russian study of 1994 asserts that more than a third of journalists have been pressured and threatened by mafiosi. A number of them have paid with their lives for critical reports on criminality and corruption. There are rumours that mafiosi are being hired by top-ranking officials.

Whereas the nation-wide press no longer reaches the provinces – except for the governmental newspaper *Rossiyskaia Gaseta* – television does and, therefore, has become the main source of information on Russian politics.

TV's ambivalent role

The most important television channel 'Public Russian Television' (ORT) is 51 per cent government-owned and controlled by the presidential apparatus. It broadcasts nation-wide and to all regions of the CIS. The second channel, 'Russian Radio and Television' (RTR), has taken a more critical stance, but broadcasts in the Russian Federation only. The third is 'TV St Petersburg'. The fourth and comparatively most critical and independent channel is 'Independent TV' (NTV). It was founded by a business tycoon eager 'to invest in future political power'.

NTV reported regularly, in a critical manner, on the war in Chechyna which may be explained by the new capitalists' opposition to adventurous policies. However, NTV lined up with all other television channels to give strong support to Yeltsin in the presidential elections of 1996 and gave a poor coverage of the Communist candidate. This was clearly not so much the result of political pressure than of the self-interest of the new capitalists to prevent the Communist leader from coming to power. Their interest was clearly shared by reform-minded journalists eager to defend a (relatively) free media.

As to the content and messages of the media, no systematic analysis is available but the headlines of 1992 about 'democracy' and 'market' have given way to fears about 'Russia's decay' and appeals to patriotism ('Russia's harmony' or 'Russia's way'). These in turn have then been substituted by nationalist slogans such as 'Russia's power' or 'Russia's leading role in the CIS' which seem to reflect (and have contributed to) the changing mood. There is also a trend towards non-political, private and personalized issues in the printed media and towards soap operas and films on television which reflects the public's increased apathy towards political affairs.

Thus, one could conclude that the media, i.e. the nation-wide free press, has lost much of the role which it played during *glasnost*, when it was a major driving force in favour of a gradual democratization of the country. While political conformity of the media could not be successfully imposed, new capitalists now control important parts of the media and, therefore, have the power to influence public opinion.

1.1.10. The public as a player in elections

Being a heterogeneous group, it is difficult to define the narrower self-interest of the public. By voting for Zhirinovsky in 1993, it provoked or accelerated the shift in foreign policy towards a more nationalistic slant, but by voting against him in the parliamentary and presidential elections in 1995 and 1996, it also demonstrated its opposition toward any kind of political extremism. By also turning down the Communist candidate, in

1996, it clearly opposed going back to the Soviet past. Apart from elections, however, the public is rather a factor which limits, to a certain extent, the scope of the actions of other players who cannot move too far beyond what is perceived as acceptable in the public's mind, at least as long as free elections are taking place. Of course, the public's mind is not constant but also dependent on the major players' propaganda and factors such as the standard of living.

1.2. THE MAIN FACTORS

What now are the main factors in the sense of collective feelings, perceived threats from the outside world, geostrategic interests and socio-economic climate, which influence different participants, apart from their pursuit of self-interest, or which may limit their scope of action?

1.2.1. Popular disorientation

What do the people think? There are as many answers as people asked, which in itself is a good sign, indicating that uniform thinking has disappeared. There is more disorientation than orientation, among individuals as well as in society as a whole. The erosion of Communist principles and the final breakdown of the Communist system have left an ideological vacuum, and the loss of the empire which was synonymous with 'Russia' has left a vacuum as to national idea and identity. This can be filled only gradually, first by redefining historic and traditional values and second by introducing influences from the outside world.

However, what exactly are these values? In reality, there is little knowledge about real values, as in Soviet times there existed no social science, and opinion polls which have become highly fashionable are hardly suited for exploring what Russians believe in, what shapes their minds and behaviour and what it means for them to be Russian.

Some Russians would say that thinking in terms of the traditionally strict social hierarchy is still very common. Standing in awe of the authorities is deeply rooted not only in the population, but also in the political élite. Pluralism is perceived more as an inevitable evil than as a value in itself. Intolerance is common. People feel that strong authoritarian rule is needed to protect the Russian land and its cultural traditions. Egalitarianism is still strong, as is resentment against private property. At the same time, this does not imply going back to the Communist system, even though the most disadvantaged groups in society (pensioners, industrial workers, the lower ranks of the state employees) do look nostalgically on the Brezhnev years as the 'Golden Era'. Not many people (and even less so the younger generations) could be made to believe any longer in a utopia about a bright future.

Others would agree, to some extent, but add that it would be too narrow-minded to attribute the present disorientation to the breakdown of the Communist ideology. Rather, Russia is in a post-totalitarian crisis. The centuries-old totalitarian trends on which the Bolshevics were able to build their power at the time of the Revolution and which reached their culmination under Stalin have broken down.

Post-Stalin socio-cultural crisis

Since Stalin, totalitarianism has been crumbling, beginning with Kruschev's 'thaw' in the 1950s and only stabilized at the surface during the Brezhnev years. During the Brezhnev period, the Communist élite's constant lying and the two-facedness of conformist behaviour in public, while different attitudes were held in private, began to spread in society, as did cynical and individualistic attitudes or aspirations to personal freedom. These years also gave birth to the rapidly growing shadow economy and to regional leaders taking liberties and ruling their provinces or districts like personal fiefdoms. In the 1980s and

1990s, finally, the socio-cultural crisis embraced the whole of Russian society. Old social groups and institutions disintegrated and the official socialist values were dismantled, leaving only candid or cynical relations among post-totalitarian/Soviet individuals.

It is said that the characteristics of the Russians' present state of mind are as follows:

- social pessimism, disappointment about the results of *perestroika*, loss of belief in quick success of transformation;
- frustration, deep concern about current events, lack of trust in the future, loss of any feeling of personal security (best reflected in the dramatic fall in birth rates);
- open and aggressive envy towards all those who are better-off and above all towards privileged groups;
- traditional paternalism and egalitarianism now further stimulated by poverty and the demeaning situation of the population at large;
- mistrust and alienation of all political institutions beginning with the old ones and ending with the new, antipathy and mistrust toward all present political leaders;
- disillusion with the market economy, democrats and democracy in general;
- alienation of everything else, of old social groups and structures, values and moral standards, feelings of help-lessness among the weak and extreme cynicism among the stronger parts of society.

Critical attitudes and self-reliance

Clearly, there are differences between the generations, those living in the big cities or in the countryside and between the adaptable and the less adaptable parts of society. Despite the present disorientation a number of explicitly anti-totalitarian values have been widely adopted in the society. People have

41

adopted a critical attitude towards everything. They have learnt painfully that they can no longer rely on the state as a provider but have to care for themselves. Critical attitudes and self-reliance, therefore, could become a major long-term driving force for a turn for the better. Since Russia can no longer be isolated from the outside world, international communication flows, increasing mobility of people and ideas, together with free media, may contribute to a gradual transformation of the Russian mind-set and inculcate democratic values.

Poor living conditions and resulting disenchantment

Others would not rule out this happening over the course of some generations, but for the time being, ordinary people feel helpless. For them the process of 'transition' means above all the gradual destruction of their living conditions: decaying hospitals, schools, sewage systems, closed or unaffordable museums, devalued salaries and pensions, no police protection. It is not only the pensioners who are affected, but also most of the industrial workers and large parts of the former middle class and intelligentsia (researchers, teachers, professors, doctors, officers, etc.). They have seen their savings destroyed by inflation, their jobs become insecure and their pay fall to an extremely low level. They now find themselves at the lower end of the social and wealth hierarchy with unscrupulous and often uneducated businessmen at the top, something which is difficult to accept for many of them. In most other countries, such social discontent and hopelessness would have resulted in social explosion, and the capacity of the Russian people to take suffering may also be limited. In any case, many observers say that the population, i.e. the reforms' losers including some of the intelligentsia, are looking out for a charismatic leader. Definitely not a new Stalin, but a person providing them with hope and trust in the future and with a new sense of purpose for the country, thus contributing to the social cohesion among this rather amorphous mass of disorientated people of today.

The current leaders seem to be aware of the public disorientation and are looking out for a positive national idea[12] with which people could identify. Or, and this may be closer to the truth, they are looking for a legitimation of the presidential authoritarian regime. The political élite seems to want to build legitimacy around patriotism – the glorification of tsarist (imperialist) Russia; the bravery of the Russian people during World War II; and the close alliance between the state and the Orthodox Church, which is at the present time more important than the state's relationship with the army, due to the bad shape of the latter.

However, on what else could a new 'social contract' and a new national identity be built? It could probably be built on some success of the present efforts to modernize the country, but as the transformation is still far from completed, no 'success stories' are readily at hand.

1.2.2. Nationalist temptations

If the new Russia is returning to the old legitimation of authoritarian power, how then can it suppress its old instinct of wanting to dominate its neighbours and gradually transform into a normal nation–state?

The Russian empire fell to pieces, all of a sudden, to the great surprise of the Russians and everyone else, including the West. Other empires decayed over decades with their centre always fighting back and instincts of domination vanishing only gradually. Should we really expect the peaceful end of the Soviet Union also to have extinguished Russian hegemonical instincts? It could be argued that this would be asking from Russia a degree of self-negation for which there is no historical precedent.

At the same time, it is true that the population simply did not

43

care about the breakdown of the empire in the first two years after the end of the Soviet Union. The Yeltsin regime could not be seen to worry about it since Yeltsin himself had accelerated it. The attitude of the population could be explained by the widely held perception that the Russian empire was exceptional, with the centre paying for the 'colonies' and not the other way round. Therefore, many believed that getting rid of them would benefit Russia and its people. Attitudes have changed since then and this is due to a number of factors:

- By mid-1994 some 2 to 2.5 million Russians living in non-Russian CIS countries had left their host countries and migrated back home (many more, some 6 to 7 million, are expected to do the same by the year 2000).

  Their host countries have re-written the history books, and in the process, they have attributed much of their desperate situation to the previous Russian domination. This has contributed to feelings of hatred against Russians and led to discrimination in terms of their professional opportunities and the use of the Russian language. Anti-Russian sentiment has been used to retain power, and the opposition has used it as an instrument to gain power and knock out political adversaries. For them it was more important to further personal political ambitions by playing the nationalist card than to think about the consequences which led to increasing economic decay, since it was the Russian minorities who ran the factories and hospitals in their host countries.[13] However, one may have to accept that the nationalist idea was and is the only one (the easiest one to understand) to fill the ideological vacuum, to mobilize society and consolidate the new nations.

  Russians living in Russia were increasingly upset about the discrimination practised against their fellow countrymen living abroad, a feeling reinforced by political propaganda. At the same time, and despite a large degree of sympathy towards the fate of the Russian minorities, the Russians at home feared that those returning would compete with them for housing and jobs.

- With the dissolution of the Warsaw Pact in 1990, some 1.2 to 1.6 million Russian soldiers and family members returned home from Central and Eastern Europe, Eastern Germany, the Baltic States, Cuba and Eastern Mongolia. The once glorious and socially respected soldiers of the Red Army, which had been a symbol of great Russian power – the Soviet Union – came back to a country in deep economic crisis and shaken by national, territorial and religious conflicts which could not offer them a life-perspective, or even modest housing. The soldiers felt humiliated, and questioned whether the government have not given up 'Russian spheres of influence' too easily. The number of returning soldiers being so huge, the population experienced their humiliation as well and began to ask the same question. Many say, therefore, that the withdrawal of troops is one of the most important factors contributing to nationalistic feelings and calls for restoring the empire and great Russian power.

- Economic decay and extreme social and psychological insecurity made people turn increasingly towards tradition, nation and religion, in short, searching for their own roots. Ambitious politicians were all too ready to fuel national feelings. In Russia, the Zhirinovskyites and the Communists played the nationalistic card, and the government adopted an increasingly nationalistic rhetoric as well. It provoked the war in Chechnya, not least because it thought that a demonstration of Russian power would be very popular.

- The nationalistic wave has provoked, since 1988–89, a series of bloody conflicts (Nagorny-Karaback, Georgia-Ossetia-Abchasia, Moldavia-Gagansia-Transnistria) which, in turn, nourished the feeling among Russians that their country had to play a 'leading role within the CIS' by stabilizing the region and preventing Yugoslavia-style conflicts. Thus, the original idea of a Commonwealth of 'equally' independent states gradually gave way to that of a leading role for Russia, and the Russian population seem to have willingly accepted this, if only because they wanted to be proud of something. And, for the time being, there may not be much else to be proud of other than Russia's immense territory and power.

- Westerners have also contributed to Russian nationalism by adopting a patronizing attitude, and Russians consider that some of their present difficulties are caused by their attempts to adapt to the Western models. There is a widely held suspicion that the West want to weaken Russia deliberately and abuse it economically, since it seems all too keen on exploiting its natural resources, and is completely ignoring Russia's cultural and scientific achievements, as well as its natural 'great power status'. Perceptions that 'Great Russia is being humiliated' feed inferiority complexes that people might wish to compensate for by feeling that they belong to a great power and a superior race. This could turn into anti-Western attitudes as well, since Russia has always suffered from an inferiority complex towards the West. It had resulted in suspicion and even animosity towards the West, at the time, which the bizarre logic of psychology has somehow translated into a superiority complex.

Growth in nationalistic feeling

We should not yet speak of animosity, but the initial positive attitude towards Westerners has given way to a perceived need to keep the distance. The period where there were hopes for a democratic Russia in a 'common European house' integrated into the world community, is now disdainfully called the 'romantic period'.

Thus, Russian nationalism is fed mainly by economic and social misery as well as by the nationalism of other CIS republics. These national tensions could become self-feeding and get out of hand. Obviously, it would have been preferable if the Soviet Union had not disappeared within those few days in December 1991, but rather after a period of restructuring which would have allowed different nationalities to find a *modus vivendi* in a spirit of peaceful co-existence and cooperation. However, people should realize that such a restructuring would hardly have been possible given the centralized political and economic system of the old Soviet Union. Nevertheless, most of the élite and the population see its disappearance as a result of political mistakes, not as something unavoidable. Not surprisingly, nostalgic feelings extend mostly to the Ukraine, Belarus and to Kazakhstan, much less so to the Baltic states and (other) southern republics.

Could nationalism turn into chauvinism or even fascism? In Russia, there has always been a tendency towards radicalism and extremism. Already, some nationalist leaders are advocating the creation of a homogeneous nation, free of 'alien elements'. Others are nostalgic of tsarist Russia with its strict hierarchy of nationalities dominated by the Russian people. We observe a still small but rapidly growing number of publications, openly propagating anti-Semitism and speaking of the Caucasian people as the 'Russian Negroes', for example.

It seems that extremist groups could also recruit among the younger generation, especially among those with bleak prospects, and there are many of them, since the reform process has also resulted in a breakdown of the Soviet education system and its socialization process. The most important state agents of socialization (kindergartens, youth groups, school, army) are in decay. The family should have to take over their role, and educate the children in social values. However, many families seem to be reluctant to accept this new role and, in addition, they are themselves disorientated. Their main form of treatment seems to be corporal punishment which has once again become widespread. Brutality continues in the street and

47

in the army which seems to make the uneducated part of the younger generation a potential breeding ground for all sorts of organizations propagating or using violence, political as well as criminal.

Violence and pacifism

Generally speaking, Russian society seems to lack a consensus on the non-use of violence. The brutalization of Russian society was mirrored in the government's behaviour towards Chechnya. Obviously, Russia's ruling class accepts violence as a political means to an end and seems to believe this is also acceptable to the people, if justified with populist arguments. Going to war with Chechnya was justified because of its being a 'safe haven for crime' and by the need to 'protect Russian citizens' living there. However, the unofficial reasons have been seen to be much more important: namely to give a strong signal to the Caucasian people that Russia considers their energy-rich region as its 'backyard' as well as its gateway to the south.

Meanwhile, Russian leaders must have realized that going to war is highly unpopular nowadays. The Russian people remember the protracted war in Afghanistan as Americans remember Vietnam. They want to live in peace. They voted down Zhirinovsky in 1995, not because he is considered foremost a ridiculous person but because of his dangerous political ideas. There is, at present, no broad chauvinist movement. However, if the efforts to modernize the country were to fail, one could not exclude a turn towards aggressive nationalism and attempts to re-build, once again, Russian 'greatness' on military power.

1.2.3. Great Power nostalgia

Russia's foreign relations aims range from a democratic Russian integration into the world community 'in accordance with its status as a great power' and with cooperative relations with its 'new neighbours', right up to an authoritarian Russia once again closing its window to the West for the next 50 years or so, dominating its 'Near Abroad' by rebuilding all or part of its former empire.

This spectrum of views, except for the 'new neighbour' element, is centuries old and it reflects the old debate between 'Westerners', 'Eurasians', 'Slavophiles', 'Great Russian imperialists' and 'Isolationists'.

'Westerners' and 'Slavophiles'

'Westerners' were mostly to be found among the intelligentsia and educated élite, while the population at large was 'Slavophile'. This had the result that all Russian attempts in history to reform and modernize the country along Western models had to be imposed from the top and, therefore, never took root within the population and, in the end, failed.

- The 'Westerners' of today look at the West as a natural ally of Russia, supporting its political and economic modernization and willing to develop together with Russia as an 'equal' partner, a new world order.
- The 'Eurasians' insist on an independent way for Russia as a multi-ethnic and multi-cultural country with its own traditions, values and interests, between Europe and Asia. The moderates in this camp would not rule out a partnership with the West, whereas the extremists fundamentally oppose Western civilization (democracy, individual rights, open market) and favour authoritarianism and the restoration of Russia, not only as a regional power, but as a world power.
- The 'Great Russian imperialists' are not far off from the extreme 'Eurasians' in their request for a clear political and moral delineation of the West. They adhere to the idea of a

'spiritually' founded Russia with a specific 'mission' (to be imposed on other people). They continue to think in terms of the Cold War and vehemently resist disarmament.

- The 'Slavophiles' are basically 'Russophiles' primarily propagating the rebuilding of parts of the empire by the unification of all Slavs under Russian leadership.

- The 'Isolationists' tend to think that, since repeated attempts by Russian rulers to import Western ideas and models have failed, Russia should concentrate on itself. The Russian continent would have enough resources to develop independently of world markets.

Great Power aspirations

The only common goal which these different schools of thought seem to share is that Russia should again become a great, influential and respected power. Russian foreign policy has always been driven by prestige thinking, but apart from this, it could be argued that Russia needs to be a strong regional power to meet the many challenges it has to face.

In Russia, foreign policy is decided on by a very small heterogeneous élite. They do not discuss foreign policy orientations theoretically in terms of 'Westerners' or 'Eurasians' (although these basic orientations also influence their perceptions of Russia's national interest) but look at Russia's geography, its geostrategic situation and interests as well as the challenges ahead. What are these?

- Although not directly a foreign policy issue, it should be underlined that Russia's first interest is to keep firmly within the *Russian Federation* the regions which are rich in energy and raw materials. Some 90 per cent of the natural resources are to be found east of the Ural mountains, while the two-thirds of Russia's population living to the west of them will need these valuable resources for their economic survival.

Hence, they could not accept any separatist policies of the eastern provinces.

- Looking at the *near abroad* and beginning with the southern border, there are the mountain people of the Northern Caucasus who are connected with each other and with Russia by old traditions of conflicts and military disputes. Russians fear that granting independence to Chechnya would trigger or amplify separatist tendencies not only in other Caucasian regions (Daghestan, Ingushia, etc.) but also in other areas of the Federation as well. They are afraid of a protracted war in the Caucasus which is considered a strategically important region, giving access to the oil-rich Caspian Sea area and to the Black Sea as well as to the Iranian world. For centuries, possession of the Caucasus was a contentious issue between Russia, Iran and Turkey, and Russia does not want the latter two to extend their zone of influence.

- Next are the *five Central Asian States* (Kazakhstan, Uzbekistan, Turkmenistan, Kyrgyzstan and Tadjikistan) which Russian geostrategists call the 'soft belly of Russia'. The best relations are those with Kazakhstan. There, Islamic fundamentalism is not significant; no foreign forces attempt to gain a dominant influence; and the large Russian population living in West Kazakhstan seems to have contributed to wise political leadership, very sensitive to Russian interests. However, in the other states ethnic tensions are growing, militant Islamism seems to be on the rise, and armed disputes could result in an eruption of violence. Russians fear their rivals of old may extend their zone of influence to these states. They perceive threats of an 'Afghanization' of Tadjikistan and other parts of Central Asia, of Iranian exportation of political Islamic fundamentalism, of pan-Turkism, and of China's pursuit of supremacy. Russia is also well aware of the increasing interest of the United States in the energy-rich region around the Caspian

51

Sea which some Western oil companies and politicians consider as the 'Persian Gulf' of the 21st century.

- To the south-east, there is densely populated *China* which Russia perceives as both a partner and a potential threat. Russia, as well as the Central Asian states of the CIS, hope to benefit from close economic cooperation with China. But the latter also fear Chinese immigration and influence. China, as well as Russia, seems interested in a certain strategic partnership as a balance to the influence of the United States. Therefore, Russia's further political and economic decline would hardly be in the interest of China, and neither would be a chauvinist Russia striving for a reintegration of the Central Asian republics and restoring Russian supremacy in the Western Pacific.

On the other hand, China is developing rapidly into an economic giant, possibly reaching the United States' gross national product by the year 2010 (though not on a per capita basis), and striving for a superpower status. Thus, China may well become the main strategic challenge for Russia. In case this risk were to turn into a threat, Russia would not have much choice but to lean toward the West and look for partnership with it. Meanwhile, it may feel most comfortable by balancing between both of them.

Russia and NATO

With a resurgent China in the south-east and a potentially aggressive Islamic world in the south, Russia is fearful of an expanding NATO in the west. However, such fears are not about being threatened but about being isolated and cut off from Europe. Many think that such fears could be overcome if NATO enlargement came along with a strengthening of the 'partnership for peace' agreement, which many Russians say in its present form neither contains much substance nor fully acknowledges Russia's status as a 'great power'.

Russia's foreign policy will mostly be driven by domestic events. There was a definite policy shift, beginning in 1993, from the views of the 'Westerners' to the (moderate) 'Eurasians'. The shift was driven by the consolidation of presidential authoritarian power, and also by the fact that the Western orientation had already brought many of the results Russia was looking for, i.e. the withdrawal from Afghanistan, the end of the arms race, the establishment of Russia as legal successor of the Soviet Union, a benevolent attitude of the West toward Russia's modernization efforts (including economic assistance) and the assurance that the West will not exploit its temporary weakness.

Russia may also have considered that the unilateral orientation toward the West was simply unbalanced and not corresponding to its geography. With its 'Eurasian' orientation, it will want to have a bigger say in world affairs. However, even communist or nationalist forces may realize (or have to realize, in the event of them seizing power) that Russia, for the time being, does not have the economic resources to play a major political role in the world. Certainly its diplomatic corps is still excellent, though many leave and turn to business. The new KGB is as powerful as the old one. The Russian Army is still a great force, and its disastrous performance in street fighting Chechnyans should not be taken as a proof to the contrary. Nevertheless, Russia lacks the resources to prevent its fleets from rusting or to modernize its strategic nuclear weapons, for example.

Russia and the 'near abroad'

At the very most, Russia would wish – to put it mildly – to influence the 'near abroad', over which it held sway for so long. Striving for greater influence and – to put it positively – to impose a *Pax Russica* is, of course, far more than a question of prestige and assertion of Russia's status as a great power. It is a question of perceived threats to its security and economic interests.

Russia wants to preserve the outer borders of the CIS (delimiting Russia's zone of influence) and is therefore pushing for the restoration of a common defence area including Russian military presence in other CIS republics. It feels a need to claim the role of a guarantor of stability and peace in this area because of the many ethnic tensions, contested borders and in order to protect the rights of the Russian minorities in the 'near abroad'. In addition, Russia has an economic interest in retaining or regaining access to or control of rich raw material and energy resources, mostly those around the Caspian Sea. Russia is also interested in regaining access to the other republics' markets for industrial goods.

The present CIS is perceived as having ensured a minimum of communication between the republics in the years immediately after the collapse of the USSR, but as completely insufficient for ensuring cooperation, not to speak of reintegration. In fact, the very numerous agreements and decisions adopted by CIS leaders have largely remained on paper since it lacks effective organizational instruments and mechanisms, but probably even more political will and power on the part of many of its leaders. Therefore, the Russian political élite seems to be keen on developing new forms of CIS reintegration, as well as new relations between Russia and the Commonwealth.

Approaches to reintegration and cooperation with former republics

It is said that for Russia, renewed integration with many former Soviet republics is almost an inevitable strategic choice, and 'the only question is when, in what form and on what conditions'. Three major approaches are discussed:

- *rebuilding the empire and Russian domination*, promoted by nationalists, communists and centrist groups. The Zhirinov-skyites prefer the use of military force, others, political and economic pressure;

54

- *Russian 'leadership' instead of direct domination*, i.e. a common market for all commercial goods, close political and military ties and common citizenship;
- *confederation of the CIS states with equal rights*, building on specific common projects (collective security, fighting crime, etc.) and with a common market as a long-term goal.

Reintegration or cooperation?

The present Russian leadership is still very cautious towards ideas of reintegration, fearing mostly the immediate economic cost for Russia.

Russia's reluctance to forge closer economic ties (i.e. monetary union) with Belarus serves to underline this argument. However, it also seems to feel that some sort of close reintegration would enhance Russia's international role, quite apart from its longer-term economic advantages. On the other hand, Russia cannot postpone for too long tougher policies towards the CIS, since time would permit the other republics to consolidate their new nationhood and develop their own national identity. Advisers to President Yeltsin rate the chances for the various republics to come back 'home' into a new Union differently: Belarus, Armenia and Kazakhstan are considered as the 'most likely' candidates; chances for a reintegration with Ukraine, Georgia and Kyrgyzstan are 'not overwhelming' but still 'considerable'; Turkmenistan, Uzbekistan and Tadjikistan are seen as 'even less likely' candidates; Moldavia and Azerbaijan 'remain to be seen'; Latvia could 'not be fully excluded', whereas Estonia and Lithuania are seen as 'being lost' for a new Union.

It would not be fair to consider all plans for closer cooperation as Russian attempts to rebuild the (Soviet) Union. All the Republics are economically strongly interdependent, since their industrialization was designed by the central 'plan' which deliberately fostered such interdependence (growing cotton in Kazakhstan and manufacturing textiles in Russia, for example) in order to ensure the cohesion of the Soviet Union. Therefore, the breakdown of the Soviet Union and trade relations could not avoid ending in economic collapse. Restoring old trade links would be helpful for all the republics, except for those which have rich energy resources (Turkmenistan, Uzbekistan, Tadjikistan and Azerbaijan) and access to world markets. They all seem to have perceived the need to build national independence on a sound economy and not solely on an own national flag. Therefore, a number of them are looking for closer economic ties with Russia, as well as for other security considerations which may be even more important (for Armenia, for example). However, what makes many of them shy off is the fear of being dominated again by Russia.

To counter such fears, Russia is proposing integration according to the model of the European Union, with equal rights for each member, no domination but adherence to commonly agreed rules. However, could one expect Russia, which dwarfs all the other CIS republics in terms of territory, population, size of army and natural resources, to submit to common rules? Somehow, this idea does not fit in with Russia's presidential authoritarian rule and its claims for a 'leading role' within the CIS. Therefore, one may expect continued reluctance on the part of the non-Russian republics towards closer integration and that Russia would gradually try to pressurize and bully its 'near abroad' back into its security orbit, at minimal cost. Cheap energy supplies would be one of its major instruments to achieve this goal.

1.2.4. Poor economic prospects

There is an abundance of Western literature about Russia's reform progress and, therefore, no need to retrace it. There are a large number of economic forecasts of which the most optimistic are presented by former Western advisers to the Russian governments. They tend to believe that the freeing of the market forces and Adam Smith's 'invisible hand' cannot but result in economic success. In comparison, Russian economists tend to be pessimistic, and optimistic only in case a huge wave of foreign direct investment were to flow into the country.

Looking at short- to medium-term prospects:

- Optimists point to the steep fall in production and argue that what has come down must go up again. However, the fall may not have been as steep as recorded by the official statistics. Rather, a part of the production seems to have been channelled into the shadow economy. Thus, production capacities may be less under-utilized than one might think and, hence, the scope for a strong recovery more limited. In addition, parts of the production capacity may have become obsolete. Despite quite successful attempts to increase arms exports, it is not conceivable for the Military Industrial Complex to reach its former production figures by producing weaponry. Neither is it realistic to assume that the MIC has sufficiently diversified away from weapons to be able to boost its production of consumer products or industrial equipment. For this to happen, it would have had to pursue strong investment activities in recent years. However, this was not the case; investment activity was, and still is, in an extraordinarily deep depression.
- Some argue that Russian production could get a boost from more exports to other CIS countries. However, most of them are in an even more miserable situation than Russia and, therefore, could not pay for Russian exports. Others think that protectionism could stop the over-abundant importation of Western goods and, thus, give a strong stimulus to domestic production. Such a proposal would immediately be denounced by Western economists as being counter-productive since it would reduce the pressure on

Russian industry to modernize. In short, there are so many ifs and whens that forecasting Russia's short- to medium-term economic development would be like reading the tea leaves. Instead of adding to speculation, we shall look at some factors which tend too often to be neglected. They suggest that Russia is not likely to become a Chinese-type boom economy, neither in the medium term nor in the longer run.

- Medium-term prospects are burdened by very serious budgetary problems. The tax system is confiscatory, and therefore tax evasion is common. There is an agreement on the need for a thorough overhaul of the whole tax system and the large financial–industrial groups may lobby strongly in favour of it since they seem to have difficulties in hiding their profits much longer. However, reform will be extremely difficult since the provinces are not too keen on establishing clear fiscal relations with the central government. Therefore, there is a serious risk that the reform will take time and that the fiscal problems will continue, the result of which could leave the central government with not much choice other than to print money. The resulting new wave of inflation would shake confidence and further push up inflation and (real) interest rates, thus adding another blow to investment aimed at the restructuring and modernization of industry.

Looking at long-term prospects, we find on the *human capital* side the following:

- On the positive side, there is a highly educated population which is keen on improving its standard of living. In addition, there seem to be hundreds of thousands of well-trained and adaptable (younger) people who have understood the opportunities which the 'transition' offers them individually and which they want and need to seize, since they have few other alternatives. Clearly, they are keen. However, not many have the start-up capital needed to run a business.

- Whether the population at large is ready rapidly to change its work ethic is a question which only future historians will be able to answer.

- Clearly hampering Russia's potential for development is the rapid ageing of the population resulting from the dramatic fall in birth rates, a phenomenon which will hardly reverse as long as personal insecurity remains so high. The record high level of drug and alcohol abuse may continue for the same reason and contribute to further reduction of work discipline, and, even more importantly, of the life expectancy for men which already has declined to a mere 57 years.

- As for the new 'businessmen', it remains to be seen whether their preference for quick deals will give way to the laborious day-to-day running of a business. Observing them gives rise to doubts, as the Protestant or Calvinist work ethics which Max Weber found to be a formula for success, do not seem to be theirs. They seem to have a preference for a luxurious life-style which may be the result of them having become rich too quickly and too easily. However, they may find managers to run their daily business.

- It is not yet clear how directors and workers whom the privatization process established as co-owners of companies will behave, whether they will develop a preference for high salaries, as was the case in the former Yugoslavia, or for retaining some of the profits for investment. However, one may expect them continually to pressurize the government for subsidies and for slow restructuring of their industry in order to avoid serious cut-backs of the work-force.

- The directors may well support such government blackmail since they lack experience in running a business in a market environment and, therefore, fear for their positions as well.

59

Looking at the *physical capital*, we find:

- Compared with China, Russia is already highly industrialized although it is producing the 'wrong' goods. Restructuring an economy and closing down some industries (notably in the Military Industrial Complex) is always much more difficult since it meets with strong resistance, different from that when building up new industries from scratch, especially in Russia. Its production sites and plants were designed by the Soviet plan, which did not take transport costs into account, nor closeness to markets, efficient energy use and the like. Closing down the huge Soviet plants is even less of a possibility as they are surrounded by whole cities, which depend solely on them. Therefore, it is an almost inevitable choice to continue to subsidize them. Since capital is in short supply, subsidies to old plants will be at the expense of restructuring them or of investments in other projects, such as infrastructure.
- Infrastructure may become a serious bottleneck for economic development; it is decaying rapidly and not much is done to stop this. This is true not only for the transport infrastructure, but also for pipework, sewage systems and the health-care infrastructure.
- The sheer size of the territory and the inadequate transport infrastructure will always favour regional monopolistic positions and, therefore, entrance barriers for new competitors will remain high, thus reducing the pressure on the established companies to modernize.

Looking at *political factors* hampering Russia's economic development, we find:

- Economic reform does not take place any more, as it did in the years 1991–92, in a sort of socio-political vacuum, but there are now strong pressure groups or individuals (such as the 'G-7') eagerly defending what they have got of the re-distribution of Russia's assets and are keen on getting even more.

- Further redistribution meets with strong competition from potential profiteers, which tends to slow it down. However, as long as there is no decision about the future owners of an industry, no one will invest in its modernization (as has been the case in recent years).

- Political decision-making is largely untransparent, clientelism is strong, and there is no effective rule of law. Corruption is rampant. Criminal organizations have penetrated most of the Russian economy. Doing business, therefore, is risky and even dangerous, deterring talented but honest people, and is frightening off foreign investors.

- There is a tendency for the provinces to develop their own legislation and economic and financial policies which threatens further to fragment Russia's legal and economic area, eventually disrupting trade flows. Such fragmentation would also be an additional deterrent to foreign direct investment.

- The Russian Army can hardly be neglected much longer. It is pushing for new weaponry to be better able to perform peace-keeping missions in the 'near abroad', but living up to the promises of 'military reform', including the establishment of a professional army, will be a costly exercise.

Signs of economic improvement

Of course, there are bright spots as well. Moscow, St Petersburg and Nijni Novgorod are booming towns. There is the incredible talent of Russians to improvise. There is enormous dynamism and much gambling for high stakes. There is the stoicism and the capacity to endure suffering of its population. However, Russia is huge and the question is whether people will remain patient until living conditions improve everywhere in the country.

One should not exclude the possibility that the economy in general will slowly improve. However, for the purpose of this paper, it is important to say that even if this were to be the case, there will not be much to be distributed to wage-earners and worker-shareholders for quite some time. This is because business needs to accumulate capital to pay for modernization; government has to invest heavily in the maintenance of the decaying infrastructure; the health service is in urgent need of investment, and so is the severely polluted environment. The scope for distribution is further limited by the continued considerable flight of capital abroad (some say that at the end of 1996, Russian capital abroad totalled some 60 billion US dollars). Thus, one may expect the Russian people not to become better off for some time, but that social inequality will continue to increase further.

1.3. INTERACTIONS OF PLAYERS AND FACTORS AND RESULTING TENDENCIES

To answer the questions raised in the introduction, what tendencies are emerging from the interplay of shaping players and factors?

1.3.1. Towards democracy or authoritarianism?

The break-away from communism, plunging the Russian society head on into a democratic future, has not worked. The historical burden is too heavy. There never existed in Russia a broad tradition of democratic thinking, parliamentarianism, civil society, rule of law and respect for it, loyalty to the Constitution, federalism or political bargaining and compromising in public. Liberal ideas never gained moral or popular appeal. In addition, there seems to have been too much change taking place at the same time for it to be digestible. People were kicked from the Communist system with its built-in social security, into a social Darwinistic Manchester type of capitalism for which they were not prepared.

- *There is more disorientation than orientation*, more alienation from everything than adherence to anything, individually as well as collectively. People feel personally insecure, even shying away from having a family. They have become very individualistic which, seen positively, also makes them very sceptical towards all sorts of political ideologies.
- *Russian society is weak and little organized.* There are no real trade unions, no strong business associations, no major civil movements; in short, there is no civil society acting as an intermediary between the individual and the 'tsar', and in which people could become organized and democracy take root. People's main preoccupation is to struggle for material survival and, therefore, they have little time to engage in and develop social networks.
- *A real multi-party system has not yet emerged.* There are strong political parties on the left and the right ends of the spectrum, but a black hole in the middle. This tendency may be a reflection of the little extent to which there is a differentiation of the society. There are a few rich forming an upper class of sorts, but a broad middle class and bourgeoisie is emerging only slowly. The some 40 percent voting share for parties in the middle is more due to Russians being disgusted with extremist political forces than to their commitment to democracy. Also, many of the 60 percent who vote for extremists or communists are probably rather expressing their discontent with present policies than out of commitment for these forces. Since the losers of reforms are likely to outnumber the winners for many more years to come they cannot be expected to support policies that benefit mostly a small minority. Therefore, there is a potential for large swings in political preferences. Despite the fact that the

63

population at large seems to be waiting for a charismatic leader promising to establish law and order (with order being much more important than law), they would not be prepared to lend support to adventurous and aggressive policies.

Present regime to consolidate

- It should, therefore, be expected that the present type of political regime will consolidate further. As it was said earlier, this system could be described as an autocratic President with the Government as an adjunct, an 'emasculated' Parliament as an annex, and a judiciary that has yet to be developed. Since it lacks effective constitutional checks and balances, it tends to establish the President (or his *kamarilla*) as the final arbiter in all sorts of disputes, making power shift still closer to the top and becoming greatly personalized.

- However, counter-forces to presidential power have emerged and seem bound to strengthen further. Regional leaders have been democratically elected which makes them less dependent on the President and adds to the power they already exert. After all, if anybody, it is they who have *de facto* physical control in the huge Russian territory. Russia's new capitalists have acquired not only considerable economic power, but now also control much of the media, rendering them strong political players. They will make use of their power for the furthering of their own interest (as demonstrated in the presidential elections in 1996). Finally, while the President continues to be the main source of legislation, his *executive* power is strongly reduced by an all-embracing corruption preventing legislation being implemented properly.

- The judiciary as well as the police and militia forces are fighting a seemingly lost battle against corruption and organized crime, and are said to be corrupt themselves. There is no effective rule of law and not too many seem to have an interest in developing one. For the time being, neither the executive nor the legislative are keen on sharing power with an independent judiciary, and the new capitalists as well and the bureaucracy seem to be interested in the preservation of the present legal grey-zone, not to mention the Mafia. However, without a rule of law including the proper implementation of legislation, democracy exists only on paper.

- None of the major players will want too strong a President. The regional leaders do not want too strong a centre, which could eventually cut back on their powers. The capitalists do not want a strong President, since they would stand to lose influence and political backing for the further extension of their economic power. Neither do those others (including the Kremlin *kamarilla*) who have some-how profited from the non-transparent privatization of Russia's wealth. If the population were to vote for a tough leader, the general interest of the public would clash with that of the new business élite. Such a development could become dangerous if the new tough leader were to rely on parts of the army to implement his policies, or simply to stay in power. The real test for Russia's democracy would come if someone who is not favoured by the new (old) élite were voted into power.

1.3.2. Towards a market economy with the capacity to integrate into the world economy?

Russia's route to capitalism is firmly established, especially since the progressive and clever part of the old élites together with some newcomers with good connections got their slice of the cake. However, large parts of the population resent capitalists (as they resent democracy). Since a marked improvement of their living standards is not (yet) in sight, but rather a further increased social inequality, hostility towards the new economic and social system may increase. Still, one should not expect social discontent to develop into violence. Russia is too huge in size for this to happen, and it lacks effective organizations with the capacity to ignite the explosives everywhere at the same time. Moreover, riots always started in big cities, and urban population nowadays votes overwhelmingly for moderate political forces (because the city-dwellers were the first to feel the benefits of a capitalist Russia).

Weak market system

However, a market system governed by clear rules and fair economic competition is not yet in sight. The dismantling of monopolies meets with strong resistance from their new owners. Anti-trust legislation meets resistance, and so does the implementation of other parts of the legal framework essential for the proper functioning of a market economy. Even more important, a market system is not possible unless there is an effective rule of law. Its absence has turned privatization into a predatory attack benefiting those with the best connections. The most influential new capitalists now form a silent alliance with the central and regional governments, fuelled by a steady flow of bribe-money and further favours in return. These alliances replace economic competition with monopolies and market structures that are suffocating the creation of social wealth, preventing the population at large from benefiting from reforms. From a historical perspective, such alliances were always, sooner or later, cohabitating with open or hidden authoritarian political systems anywhere in the world.

The prospect that Russia would integrate in the world economy (soon) is unlikely. The submission of Russia to international economic rules and keeping it open to international competition would challenge and reduce the power of the silent alliance. The latter would not want this, but would prefer monopolistic and corporatist structures as well as interventionist policies, which have to be shielded from the outside world. Therefore, increasing protectionism is much more likely; even more so as the earlier submission of Russia to international economic rules and keeping it open to rapid opening–up and the overflow of the Russian market with foreign goods are now being perceived as having contributed directly to the fall of production. Furthermore, the protectionist option may be all the easier as Russia would not have to fear too much from its trade partners in terms of retaliation. Besides energy and some raw materials (and weapons), it does not produce many products which the Western world would want to buy. Nevertheless, protectionism would shorten the political agenda for a constructive dialogue with the West, and complicate relations between Russia and the Western world.

1.3.3.   A nation respectful of its new neighbours or an empire again?

Russia is striving for control of the post–Soviet space which is perceived as being Russia's legitimate zone of influence. The post–Soviet space is considered as Russia's defence area with the outer republics serving as buffers to Russia's security. Lacking the material basis for playing the role of a superpower, Russia will at least remain a strong regional power and it might need to be one, since there are many potential conflicts. In the south, Russia wants to ward off Islamic fundamentalism and Turkish influence. Along the southern border of the CIS, new economic and potentially strong military powers are emerging. Many of the borders with the newly independent states (as well as between them) are arbitrary and potentially contentious. Russia wants to protect the 25 million compatriots living in the 'near abroad'. A protectionist Russia will also need the other republics to follow similar economic policies since it is not able to control its borders with them. Finally, Russia seems to realize that it does not have many friends in the world and will therefore attempt to forge a closer alliance with those it knows best.

The Russian Army is keen on a new role enhancing its prestige and social status. Becoming the guardian of a sort of *Pax Russica* could serve this purpose. Russia's capitalists want access to neighbouring countries' energy and raw material resources as well as to their markets. The Russian Orthodox Church considers the post–Soviet space as its spiritual zone of influence, although it tolerates Islam in the south. The national mood seems to favour a 'leading role' for Russia in the CIS, a mood propagated by the Presidency.

Some of the republics are looking for closer relations with Russia, especially those with few economic resources or those with such a geographic position that they are left with little choice other than accept belonging to the zone of Russian influence. They seem to have realized that independence cannot be built on a national flag, but requires a sound economy and positive relations with the regional leading power. To alleviate the fear of being dominated again, Russia is propagating an integration along the model of the European Union. However, Russia does not want to be integrated, but rather seeks to integrate others into its realm. Therefore, most of the republics refrain from establishing closer ties with Russia. Since time works in favour of the CIS republics' consolidation into nation–states, Russia will probably step up its efforts to pressure and bully (some of) the republics firmly back into its security orbit. Cheap energy supplies would be the main instrument for achieving this goal, not open aggressiveness.

Despite the fact that the Russian desire to rebuild its empire is dependent on the reintegration of Ukraine (considered part of the Russian heartland), such a union would be very different from the former Soviet Union as the same level of economic and political centralization would with near certainty be impossible to attain.

1.3.4.   Russia occupied by internal reform or threatening to the outside world?

For the time being Russia will continue to be occupied by internal developments, since its revolution is not yet over. Its society is still in a state of flux, and so are its political institutions. New social classes are emerging; social tensions seem bound to grow, and further ethnic conflicts cannot be excluded. The reforms undertaken and inspired by Western models will need to be further adapted to Russia's own traditions, peculiar characteristics and to the power balance between the main influential players.

Based on present tendencies, Russia will not threaten its 'near abroad' nor the rest of the outside world. The population at large wants to live in peace and the younger generations are not keen to mobilize for military adventures; neither the regional leaders nor the new capitalists would support aggressive policies as they would rather seek to further consolidate their power; and finally, the Russian Army is in bad shape.

Russia may also travel different routes. Chapter 2 presents scenarios for some of the possible alternative futures for Russia.

Notes

1 President Yeltsin himself may serve as the best example, starting as a radical reformer and the personification of democratic hopes in 1985 and adopting progressively, since 1993, national–authoritarian attitudes. By the end of 1993 he had replaced all his democratic-minded advisers by *power maniacs* of the police and security forces loyal to him only. Parallel to this, his rhetoric shifted from terms like 'democracy', 'rule of law', 'human rights' towards national imperial authoritarian terms such as 'Russia's power', 'Russia's leading role in the CIS', 'Russia's national mission' and so on. This clearly illustrates the changing mood among the Russian élites, and Yeltsin's efforts to adapt to it in order to stay in power.

2 President Yeltsin defended the political structures as follows: 'What do you expect? In a country which is used to tsars and great leaders, in a country in which no influential interest group has yet developed, in which the representation of specific interests has not been organized, in which only today normal political parties are developing, in a country in which executive discipline is very weak – would you like to place the main burden on the Parliament of such a country? After a year, if not earlier, the people would call for a dictator. Such a dictator is easily found … In a democratic state, every period has its own balance of power. In Russia today this balance swings towards the President.' (*Iswestja*, 16.11.1993)

3 Its former Chief, General Korshakov was considered as the *éminence grise* and it was said 'that he decides everything in the Kremlin', and 'that in order to drag through a doubtful decision or sign an illegal decree' one had to go to him. He was replaced by General Lebed in June 1996 who, however, was dismissed once he had successfully performed his duty, which was to make his voters support Presi-dent Yeltsin's re-election.

4 Western analysts tend to underestimate this issue since in our countries the basic distribution of wealth is rarely discussed, having been long since decided on, and the focus is on the distribution of the *increase* of income and wealth. Still, Western economists think that money makes the world go round. This is even more true when the (re-)distribution of the total *existing* wealth is at stake. In fact, the privatization process was nothing less than an annulment of the October Revolution of 1917.

5 The term 'armed forces' includes, in addition to the troops subordinated to the Ministry of Defence, force structures sub-ordinated to other commands. All of them are directly responsible to the President, *not* to the government. These include:

- the Interior Troops of the Ministry of the Interior (some 350,000 men),
- the Border Guards (some 50,000 men, with plans to increase their number to 250,000),
- the Railroad Police and the Police Militia (number unknown),
- the Presidential Security Service (some 40,000 troops),
- the former KGB troops (some 140,000).

The armed forces subordinated to the Ministry of Defence number up to 2.3 million men. Official figures differ rather strongly!

6 This action dissolved the Congress of People's Deputies. The fact that (parts of) the Russian Army finally intervened may be explained by close personal ties between the President, or his advisers, and some military leaders. The fear of Russia slipping into anarchy and of centrifugal forces working towards the disintegration of Russia were also factors. However, many officers kept out of the conflict.

7 Privatization by distribution of 'vouchers' to workers and company managers as well as the subsequent 'insider' privatization (to banks and other financially strong groups) covered only a part of Russia's economic assets, leaving much still to be distributed, especially land.

8 It is said that the seven largest groups, which the Russians ironically call the G-7, now control half of the Russian industry, which makes them very powerful economically *and* politically. These groups financed President Yeltsin's election campaign, for which they were rewarded with the appointment of some of their representatives to high government positions, giving them access to insider knowledge and participation in decision-making. The recent decision (November 1996) to sell Russian telecommunications to some of these groups and stop the original plan of involving foreign investors, is revealing of their increasing influence and of their protectionist instincts.

9 In Moscow, Chechnyans seem to specialize in protection money, blackmail and car theft. Azeris control the drug market and Georgians prostitution.

10 The mid-left 'Rybkin Block', initiated by President Yeltsin, proved to be a failure; the social-liberal camp is split; and the radical democrats who have been the main driving force of *glasnost* politics, a rapid transformation towards a market economy and a Western-type democracy, are discredited by the economic crisis (none of these numerous parties could pass the 5 per cent hurdle in the parliamentary elections of 1995); other democrats are split as well or lack any nation-wide organization (as, for example, G. Yavlinsky's party 'Yabloko').

11 Lying behind such attitudes is the belief that there is only one truth

and that politics is just as committed to it as are philosophy and religion. Political infighting always took place behind closed doors, hidden behind a thick veil of secrets, and once a consensus was reached, the leadership (and society) behaved along the lines of either-or, friend or foe. Potential conflicts were dealt with accordingly, either by destroying the enemy (Stalin's preferred way) or delaying conflicts and sweeping them under the rug (Brezhnev's preference, leading to sclerosis of the country).

12 In August 1996 President Yeltsin launched a competition for such a national idea.

13 Ethnic nationalism is paradoxically meant as a defence against the stronger, but at the same time it turns against the weaker. Different republics want to be independent from Moscow but do not want to respect national rights of minorities in their own territory (for example, the Georgians turned against the Abchasians and Ossetians; the Lithuanians against the Poles; the Moldavians against Russians).

Chapter 2

====

Scenarios for Russia: the year 2000 and beyond

2.1. SCENARIOS FOR RUSSIA

Which way might Russia go?

Too many uncertainties exist for there to be definite answers to this question. We shall, therefore, develop a number of scenarios which describe alternative paths that Russia may take in the future. So we shall consider Russia in the year 2000 and beyond.[1]

The scenarios are comprehensive in that they focus on the whole of Russia's socio-economic and political landscape. They need to do so since a country's future depends on developments in all its spheres of activity, not only in a limited number of them.

The key variables which have been selected to describe the Russian landscape are:

- *the political setting*, i.e. the type of government;
- *the role of the armed forces and enforcement agencies* which cannot (yet) be considered an integral part of the government but may play a role of their own;
- *economic development*, which will be highly important for social stability;

- *the mind-set, the social climate and the cohesion of Russian society*, which will impact upon political developments;
- *Russia's orientations towards the outside world*, which will also reflect the outside world's attitudes towards Russia.

The scenarios that we obtained are consistent in that they link the type of government with the economic development or social climate which seems to really fit, and vice versa. Of course, this depends on expert judgement and, depending on the experts consulted, one may arrive at different links and, consequently, different scenarios.[2]

2.1.1. Bases for scenarios

It is most important that the scenarios be relevant, i.e. they have to be based on solid information. We have based ours on the *Shaping Actors, Shaping Factors* study, which attempted to put aside events or actual happenings without longer-term significance and concentrate on the underlying structural laws and their eventual change which will ultimately determine the deeper social and political undercurrents. Other sources of information were added to it. We further analysed the driving and braking forces for the different scenarios expected to materialize, which served as another test of their relevance. This analysis was also important in assessing the dynamics and sustainability of the scenarios over time and in determining within which time horizon the different scenarios may be most relevant.

2.1.2. Which scenario is relevant?

However, the question of which scenarios are most relevant, cannot be answered clearly, since this would amount to making a prediction, which is impossible.

In the end, the most important contribution of scenarios is that, thanks to their comprehensiveness and consistency, they require potential developments in one sphere of activity to be interpreted as part of a greater picture (for example, while certain economic reforms look feasible on paper, Russia's socio-political realities may render them impossible to implement). They invite the consideration of alternatives and their respective implications. They can serve as a structure for discussions with experts and so contribute to a purposeful, regular updating of information. In short, scenarios should be considered as a useful tool for informed speculation about Russia's future – no more and no less.

This chapter is organized as follows:

- The first section argues that Russia's return to Communism is not a viable option and, therefore, can be dismissed in this scenario exercise.
- Then, each scenario is presented briefly and in a condensed form. The forces working in favour or against its realization are commented upon.
- After this presentation, some ideas are presented regarding which scenarios seem likely to be more relevant over the next few years and which may be relevant only in the more distant future.
- Finally, the major findings are summarized.

2.2. WHY RUSSIA WILL NOT REVERT TO COMMUNISM

2.2.1. The Communist system cannot be revived

This paper was written in May 1996, when the Presidential elections were approaching and nervousness about a possible Communist victory was on the increase. Our reasoning was that, although this could not be excluded, it was highly unlikely to imply a come-back of the Communist system. The reasons given are still valid and will be so for the next elections.

The Communist Party is itself split

On the one hand, there is the Bolshevik wing, consisting of the most unreformed members of the old Communist Party. During *glasnost* and *perestroika*, they opposed the extension of civil liberties and the pluralization of the political system under Gorbachev, just as they opposed privatization and marketization under Yeltsin. On the other hand, there is a more social-democratic wing, favouring a greater role for the state with mixed ownership and market economy, and purportedly also accepting free elections and political pluralism. However, judgement must be reserved on the depth of these new commitments until such time (if it arrives) as the Communist Party has won control of both the executive and the legislative and is subsequently faced with presidential or parliamentary elections it is likely to lose. In any case, a party speaking with many voices is unlikely to be able to reimpose on people an ideology which comes close to a religious belief, even less so as its most ardent propagators are known to have always belonged to the mediocre levels of the former *nomenklatura* (Zyuganov, for example), whereas its higher-ranking members (like Yeltsin or Chernomyrdin) rejected the Communist philosophy.

People are no longer prepared to believe in a 'shining future'
for which present sacrifices are thought worthwhile

Russians have already experienced too much hardship in recent years and what they want is not a rosy and distant future, but an improved standard of living in the short term.

In addition, and thanks to *glasnost* permitting freedom of speech and publication, Russians have found out about the crimes committed by the *ancien régime* and the many *Gulag Archipelagos*. They have also learned about the privileges it granted to its leaders and, thus, the permanent betrayal of the ideal of equality which underpinned Communist ideology.

People now well appreciate that their former leaders were more united by their common interest in career advancement than by shared views or ideological convictions as Communist party propaganda had made out, and as many outsiders chose to believe at the time.

Yet, there are still many people looking back with nostalgia, mostly to the Brezhnev years (the 'golden era'). They may do so out of ideological conviction, or out of wanting to protect themselves psychologically by not admitting that they were betrayed and lied to during the whole of their lives without realizing what was going on. Others may look back with nostalgia to a time when they enjoyed a considerable degree of security and during which it was possible for them to fulfil a number of ambitions for their families and for themselves – which is clearly not achievable for most of today's Russians. In addition, it is undoubtedly so that egalitarian attitudes and a view of the state as the main provider are still common today. However, such attitudes are clearly not sufficient to allow a revival of the Communist ideology and system.

Moreover, the part of the population opposing the return to Communism is anything but negligible. The younger generations and the more adaptable of the older generation do not share nostalgic feelings and are becoming ever more aware (or have already learned) that they must rely on their own initiative and resources. Indeed, over half of Moscow's and St Petersburg's voters backed the democratic parties in the last parliamentary elections (which, however, is not yet a guarantee of them supporting democracy!).

How, then, would it be possible once more to impose an ideology on a population whose more astute and dynamic members (including the larger part of its former and present élites) have rejected it? Bringing back the 'Communism of old' would require extreme brutality on the part of Russia's future leaders: without an atmosphere of fear and extensive purges, new democrats and free-marketeers would not be forced into

77

submission. A return to Communism would imply, moreover, the reimposition of the state apparatus and effectively necessitate the extension of that fortress to encompass all of the CIS. For unless this were achieved, Russia, with its uncontrollable borders, would still be open to the flow of Western information and culture (it is even questionable whether this flow can be interrupted at all in this age of high-technology communications). In addition, Russia never could or would be ready to isolate herself from the rest of the world without first having brought back her 'near abroad' successfully into the fold. She has few friends in the world and, therefore, would want to be associated with those she knows, even if they would not like it.

In essence, therefore, a return to Communism would entail a corresponding return to the siege mania of the pre-*glasnost* Soviet Union. Such aggressive policies, which might easily result in bloodshed, cannot be pursued under the banner of the Communist ideology. They would require instead a new banner, whether chauvinistic or outright national-socialist, but an ideology which above all enjoys popular support. Russia's Communist leaders are fully aware of the lack of attraction of their ideology, which is one of the main reasons for their passionate appeals to Russian patriotism and nationalism.

The Communist ideology cannot be revived for economic reasons, except at the cost of brutality and bloodshed

A mixed economy with large state-owned companies and some private small and medium-sized enterprises adding some flexibility to the economy, as envisaged and practised already by Lenin's New Economic Policy (1921–28), might have been compatible with the Communist ideology. However, with privatization having gone so far ahead, a strong and influential business class has developed, that takes its decisions independently of the state, and which is effectively already in control of the national economy. Such a development is clearly not compatible with an ideology that requires total submission to the state. Doing it the Chinese way, by maintaining the Party's right to political leadership but allowing for economic freedom, is obviously no longer a possibility, once the Party has abandoned power, as is the case in Russia.

Nevertheless, it is clear that were the Bolshevik hard-liners to gain a decisive victory over the advocates of a mixed economy, they would attempt to stamp out this new class of Russians. Such a step would amount to declaring war on Russia's capitalists, the corrupt bureaucracies, the majority of the former *nomenklatura* and the regional leaders, including the Mafias; in short, all those who have profited from privatization. These people, however, have amply demonstrated their lack of moral reservations in dividing up Russia's wealth between them, and they now see an opportunity in establishing themselves and their families as the financial aristocracy and bourgeoisie of modern Russia. Therefore, it is clear that they would fight back with all means if the Bolsheviks tried to turn back the clock.

Thus, with the disappearance of the ideological, economic and institutional pillars of the Communist system, it would be exceedingly difficult to rebuild them. If an attempt were made to reintroduce a Communist system by force, it would either fail or it would succeed only in the short term, until counter-forces were to organize themselves in opposition.

2.2.2. What would happen if people voted Communist?

A majority of Russians may still vote for the Communist leader Zyuganov

This would not necessarily be because they wanted to go back to a political system in which there was only one candidate, a political discourse in which there was only one acceptable line,

79

and an economic system in which Russia chronically and abysmally failed to match the living standards of Western Europe. Rather, they would vote for him to express their deep, dissatisfaction with post-Communist hardship and uncertainty, rampant crime, public disorder and tremendous social inequality, and some may be attracted by his promises to restore Russian 'greatness'. It would mostly be the older generations or the very many losers in the reform process who would lend him their support.

Supposing Zyuganov were elected, what could he deliver?

He may slow the pace of reform further, follow more interventionist policies and invest in a social safety net for the poor (which is an urgent task anyway). He may also re-nationalize some of the more recent privatizations, those which smell most of corruption and clientelism.

Later, he might privatize them again for the benefit of his own clients, to pay off the most influential Bolsheviks. This may even become one of his (hidden) domestic national priorities, as his higher-ranking fellow party-members are hungering to participate in Russia's privatization: presently, in Russia more than in any other country in the world, political power remains the surest way to personal enrichment. Furthermore, feeding these people may contribute to changing their political convictions and bring them closer to the liberal-centrist camp.

In other words, he could follow a rather moderate line of policy which, however, is unlikely to be successful, i.e. deliver the 'social stability' for which he was voted into office. However, he would run the risk of losing his supporters to the Zhirinovskys of Russian politics, if he decided to run elections in four years' time, which, given the circumstances, seems rather unlikely.

Zyuganov might adopt a tougher line of policy as well. We

actually do not know what he really stands for and if his rhetoric is just propaganda. However, if he ever tried to follow a Bolshevik policy, with intensive re-nationalization and aggressive policies towards the 'near abroad', it is questionable whether the present state apparatus, including the armed forces and enforcement agencies, would submissively follow his instructions. Undoubtedly, he would have to purge the state machine, but could he count on a sufficient number of willing aides? As argued above, one should expect a rapidly growing resistance towards returning to a 'Communism of old'.

While Russians may vote for Zyuganov, his actual coming to power is still another question

Few Russian observers seem to believe that Yeltsin and/or his *kamarilla* would voluntarily hand over power. Yeltsin fought the Communist hard-liners in the Gorbachev era; he defeated them, standing on a tank, in the August *putsch* of 1991; he shelled their fortress, the White House, with artillery in October 1993. Could one really expect him to accept a late victory of the Communists, and over him personally? After all, such a victory would not be a normal swing of the political pendulum, as in Western democracies, but it would represent a transfer of nearly unlimited presidential power tailored for him personally, without noteworthy checks and balances, to his deepest enemies. Indeed, this would require from Yeltsin a degree of self-sacrifice which is not apparent.

Furthermore, Yeltsin's *kamarilla* would not only stand to lose their rank and influence, if he were to leave office. They seem to have been deeply involved, at least some of them, in all sorts of legal or illegal activities (what does it matter, since they make the laws!) with a view to personal enrichment. They could hardly expect to be allowed to withdraw peacefully to their *dachas* and Swiss bank accounts. Therefore, one might expect them to resist leaving their positions. Of course, this is speculation. However, it may be useful to remember Yeltsin's personal command over the powerful secret service, and some 340,000 troops (among which 40,000 élite troops, fully loyal, it seems); in addition, the Ministry of the Interior's troops and the normal military are subordinated to him, though not much is known about their eventual loyalty.

It need not and probably will not go that far. As Stalin said, with reference to voting: 'It does not matter how people vote. What is important is how you count the votes.' It would seem, therefore, that should Zyuganov win a majority, we may never know about it. However, in any event, rumours about manipulation, refusal to accept election results and hand over power, or a postponement of second-round elections, would be a heavy, even fatal, blow to Russian democracy.

2.3. FIVE SCENARIOS FOR RUSSIA'S FUTURE

2.3.1. Muddling through

The muddling through scenario

> *The President lacks a clear vision on where to lead the country and/or the capacity to take it there.*

The President's constitutional power is permanently challenged by different élites and power structures. Even his own apparatus tends to take liberties with his power. Consequently, the political system seems to be more of an 'oligarchy' than a presidential rule, and the permanent struggle for power and compromise prevents clear policy priorities from emerging.

The legal system does not work in practice and not much is done to improve it. Misuse of the judiciary is always possible. 'Law and order' is more of a slogan than an effective policy. Consequently, the Mafia gains more influence in all spheres. Information flow from the West continues, but there are occasional and increasing attempts at censorship.

Relations between the centre and the regions are negotiated *ad hoc*, and there are no serious attempts to create a clear legal framework for those relations. Ethnic or other conflicts are discouraged by the threat of military force.

Although officially subordinated to the President, the armed forces and enforcement agencies are beyond full political control.

There is no monolithic officer corps but a number of *éminences grises* which have a direct influence on Presidential/political decision-making. Before using the power structures, the President has to negotiate with its élites.

Muddling through also characterizes economic policies.

Further reforms meet strong resistance from increasingly powerful interest groups; there is no effective support for military-industrial conversion and land-reform. Old monopolies are not dismantled, nor are new ones prevented from developing.

Russia's scientific and technological potential is far from being fully used; it does not find its way into factories. The service and trade sectors continue their strong growth and create new employment, but, at the same time, hidden unemployment in the large monopolies is further increasing. The economy as a whole is growing only very slowly and business is struggling successfully to maintain a protectionist environment.

The Mafia's influence continues to grow, which also prevents the emergence of norms of business ethics and greatly discourages foreign and even national private investment.

High interest rates prevail, there is a lack of start-up capital and monopolistic/corporatist entrance barriers also exist.

A middle class is developing only very slowly, as a result of the fear of being exploited and threatened by the Mafia. Income gaps continue to widen between the few new rich and the vast majority of the population, and also between urban and rural areas. Social welfare continues to deteriorate as does the health system.

Disorientation, apathy and passivity are deepening among the population.

The gap between the population and the political élites is further widening, leading to a strong alienation from political life. Self-interest and individual survival become key personal objectives, leaving little time to engage in the networks of a civil society.

People feel deeply insecure. The past is in part rejected, and in part looked upon with nostalgia – mostly so for its connection with social protection. There is no national project, no ideology or even personality which people trust. Social and political polarization is on the increase, along with personal despair among the very many losers of the reforms.

Russia is, above all, inward looking.

It concentrates on preserving the Russian Federation, using its *de facto* dominating position to bully and pressurize the other CIS republics back into its security orbit. It establishes closer (economic) ties with Belarus, Kazakhstan, Ukraine and neglects the others, at least those with poor natural resources. It wants to control the post-Soviet space but at minimal cost. It looks for tolerably good relations with the West, but staunchly defends its national interest and resorts to arm-twisting on different issues, in an attempt to hide its Cold War defeat and give a boost to national pride.

Driving forces

In this scenario, the major driving force is the new ideology of *fast enrichment* or *rampant capitalism*. However, fast enrichment is not that new, but dates back to the Brezhnev years, when nothing in Russia worked any more without patronage, old boys' networks and cash. Thus, this scenario is a continuation of a 20-year-old preoccupation of large parts of the establishment, hidden before but legal now, which makes it all the more powerful a force.

Rampant capitalism, that is, the absence of clear legislation, implementation of it, administrative procedures and market regulations, best fits the interests of all those profiting from it, i.e. business people, well-positioned and corrupt bureaucrats including military commanders (selling weapons or other equipment), politicians, regional leaders, the crafty part of the younger generations especially in the big cities, not to speak of the Mafia.

With their further enrichment, the new capitalists extend their control over the economy, making the government increasingly dependent on them and their interests. Western historical experience would suggest that once a majority of them feels satisfied with what they have got out of the distribution of Russia's existing wealth, they will push for establishing a rule of law, protecting their property, entrepreneurial freedom and a private sphere and, possibly, also clear rules for the market economy. That is, they may develop a self-interest in domesticating capitalism's wildness and the Mafia may become (even more) interested in turning to serious business. However, it is impossible to say when the time will be ripe for this to happen, or whether it will at all. Russia has no tradition of reforms pressured for from the bottom; they have always been imposed from the top including *glasnost, perestroika* and the present Constitution (which, according to many, was not adopted with the required majority in December 1993).

Still, history may not be a reliable guide to the future: the historical paradigm may be changed by the very fact that, for the first time in Russian history, there is inheritable private property which owners want to see protected by an effective rule of law.

Concentration of capital

However, if rule of law and market regulations do not emerge, Russia might well see an ever-increasing concentration of capital in the hands of a very few, who dominate its economy and will, sooner or later, also want to dominate its political life.

So a type of Brazilian capitalism and oligarchy (in its earlier form) may emerge:

- New capitalists are making enough money from exporting the country's huge reserves of raw materials and energy to afford every luxury for themselves and still be able to finance the state apparatus. Instead of painfully modernizing industry to enable it to compete in the world market, they would let it decay and import what is needed.
- People living in the countryside would somehow have to care for themselves. In the big cities, the government would eventually subsidize the masses' living standards at just above subsistence level. This tremendous social inequality need not end up in an explosion of social disorder if both police and Mafia brutally maintain order.
- By outward appearances, a democratic system would be maintained, with different members of the oligarchy taking turns in the leadership of the country. Some generals of the armed forces would be part of the oligarchy; however, this would not result in major efforts to modernize and strengthen the army, as the rich people may not want to pay for it and the poor would not be able to. Instead, the oligarchy may stoically accept the naval and air forces

becoming obsolete, resulting in a diminution of Russia's military influence in the *far* abroad, but less so in the *near* abroad, since the other CIS republics are even weaker, economically and militarily. Russia would pressurize some of them back into its security orbit to be shielded, to some extent, from the *far* abroad.

Braking forces

Such a development would be the extreme and longer-term outcome of muddling-through policies. However, braking forces may start to work much earlier and probably would need to, if the dynamics of the process is to be stopped.

Firstly, and this can be observed since the parliamentary elections of December 1993, rampant capitalism drives the very many losers of the reform process to the *Red-Brown* camp. Unless a marked improvement in their living standards could be achieved, this could end up in a victory of the Communists first, and if they were to pursue muddling-through policies too, in a victory of the Browns later, provided, of course, that free and fair presidential elections were to take place. So rampant capitalism seems to lead to a more authoritarian regime and, thus, to another scenario.

Secondly, if rampant capitalism continued (with a more authoritarian regime), economic logic may well work in favour of the Brazilian type of capitalism. Strong exports of raw materials and energy could, in fact, result in an overvalued currency, which, in combination with free trade, would risk destroying Russian industry. In an economy without any legal framework effectively governing economic competition, for example, there would be a natural tendency for monopolies and super-rich oligarchies to emerge. To some extent, this is presently happening. However, it is very unlikely that this tendency will extend to the Brazilian extreme.

Russia's history as a great power

In contrast to Brazil, Russia has always considered itself, and actually was since the middle of the 18th century, a great power (even a world power during the main part of the 20th century). Psychologically, it could never accept being degraded to the status of a supplier of raw materials to the industrial world and China or other emerging industrialized countries in the latter's orbit, even less so as its population was proud of the country's technological achievements. Rationally, it could never accept such a role since it would effectively be marginalized in the emerging multi-polar world in which the power of the old and new poles builds on both the capacity to project force and economic strength. Were Russia to abandon its industry, the only way to maintain its influence and its scientific and technological base would be the production of sophisticated weapons. However, there is no guarantee that a Brazil-type selfish oligarchy would be ready to finance a military-industrial complex. Thus, the country's technological assets could decay and Russia could fall back to the status of a developing country, though one with an immense stock of weapons, albeit out-dated ones. This may invite quite a number of powers to extend their zone of influence, mostly the overpopulated and energy-hungry ones. In the extreme, they might consider Russia (or rather Eurasia) as the undiscovered continent or the Americas of the 21st century.

Such a long-term perspective would almost certainly cause an early and strong reaction to stop decline and marginalization. The security and foreign policy establishment would increasingly push for it. Continued economic weakness over the coming years and, therefore, perceptions of Russia eventually needing decades to modernize its economy, could accelerate it. And so might the President's perceptions of the new capitalists becoming too strong and therefore a challenge to his power. A shift in policy may be further accelerated by social unrest or disorder, which could happen even though stoicism seems to be a kind of religion in Russia, and part of the national consciousness. People may well not want to further accept their country's (natural) resources being handed over to unscrupulous speculators taking advantage of their connections, and to see their industry closed down, destroying their hopes for a better life. While it is true that trade unions presently have no power at all (except for that of the miners), one cannot exclude resistance growing and somehow becoming organized. And it is questionable whether the armed forces, discontented themselves, would be ready to stamp out riots or an explosion of disorder. Therefore, it seems that rampant capitalism in its extreme Brazilian variant is not a viable scenario.

Russia may react as it has done on several occasions in its history: after opening its window to the West and attempting to modernize the country, it may close it again and rebuild its military power. Or it may shelter behind protectionist barriers, try to catch up economically and, at the same time, invest in its military security. In either case, it may want to have the other CIS republics firmly back in its economic and security orbit.

2.3.2. Benign authoritarianism

The scenario of a benign authoritarian President

> *The President has a clear vision of transforming Russia into a functioning market economy, a state of law and a democracy.*

The President dominates the presidential apparatus by granting privileges, which in turn effectively ensures his control of the government. He enjoys the support of the élites, for his vision and his rule.

The President strongly invests in and supports an increasing role for the judiciary, thus contributing to the development of a rule of

89

law. He pursues a moderate law and order agenda. However, the results are not sufficient to reduce the influence of the Mafia.

He permits freedom of the media and resorts to censorship only in difficult situations. Thus, he allows democratic values to spread.

He negotiates the centre's relations with the regions on an ad hoc *basis*, taking account of their needs, and increasingly attempts to implement the Russian Federation Treaty effectively or to replace it with a new one. Ethnic or other conflicts in the regions are discouraged or controlled by clear conflict settlement procedures and, if need be, by police or armed force interventions.

> *The armed forces and enforcement agencies are loyal to the Constitution, accept the primacy of politics, but refuse to be used for partisan purposes.*

They are reluctant to resort to military solutions in the 'near abroad' and beyond, and are opposed to being drawn into internal conflicts.

> *The benign President starts a new type of radical economic reform.*

He overrides resistance from all sorts of interest groups and pushes ahead with the establishment of the legal and institutional framework required for a market economy. He goes ahead with de-monopolization, privatization, the conversion of the military–industrial complex and land reform. He also pushes hard for a more effective exploitation of available technical knowledge, reforms the civil service and actively fights corruption.

Special attention is paid to the encouragement of business start-ups and the development of a large middle class which he expects to become an anchor for the rule of law and democratic stability. A social network is built.

In the medium and longer term these policies pay off in terms of higher economic growth, enhanced by Russian flight-capital returning home and considerable foreign investment. New radical reforms could hamper the economic links with less reform-minded CIS republics, but Russia might encourage them to quicken the pace of reform by conditionally offering cheaper energy.

The President uses a patriotic rhetoric, creates new national symbols and tries to win over the population for his national project of modernizing Russia.

He inspires faith amongst the people, strengthening their national pride and social cohesion. In this way, moderate national consolidation is achieved.

The President wants Russia to become a positive partner integrated in world institutions.

He wants it to be accepted as a partner equal with the US, a great power in international peace and security arrangements and constructively involved in the broader European architecture. Increasingly, as Russian economic competitiveness allows, he negotiates its integration in the world economy and institutions. Relations with the other CIS countries would be constructive, but also reflect, to some extent, Russia's *de facto* dominant position in the CIS.

Driving forces

In this scenario, the President himself is an important driving force. He is a democrat by conviction, but feels that the gradual democratization and economic modernization of Russia is an immense task, asking for a long-lasting effort which could hardly be generated and maintained within a political system potentially leading to changes in the presidency every four years. Therefore, he may look for a Russian model of guided democracy, allowing for greater continuity in the leadership and for more transparency and influence of the élites in decision-making. This could well bring him the support of large parts of the élite and population, among both of whom feelings of Russia needing a strong state and strong rule, especially in times of crisis, still predominate.

Popular preoccupation would oblige the President to gently play the nationalist card. It is, in these times of general disorientation, the only national philosophy appealing to the masses with their huge patriotic potential. By doing so, he would contribute to society's cohesion, and with his national project of thoroughly modernizing the country, he would mobilize Russia's energy and rebuild its self-esteem. Thus, the President would appeal to traditional Russian values and take advantage of the present psychological climate (disorientation) to give the country a new sense of purpose, worth working for.

So the President could not impose Western models as the radical democrats did in 1991–93, but he would have to link them somehow with Russia's specificity, its actual needs and traditional values. With market economy and private property having become synonymous with wild capitalism and the 'theft' of national resources, the President would have to persuade people that private property can also serve public wealth and be a source of productivity. And with the collectivist mentality and egalitarian traditions deeply entrenched, a free, Anglo-Saxon style market economy does not seem to be a possibility for decades to come. Rather, the President would lean towards social democratic ideas combining private with state-owned property and market economy with social protection. This may run counter to economic efficiency and performance but such policies would be politically and socially sustainable, that is, they would contribute to a new social consensus or social contract.

The President's agenda for economic reform would not be able to run much ahead of what the powerful business class would be prepared to accept. In this way, the more far-sighted and influential elements of that élite would effectively set the pace for reform, but they would do so behind the scenes. The President and these sections of the business élite would then have to rise to the challenge of persuading their more backward contemporaries that they must sacrifice some of their present privileges (subsidies, monopolies, opaque privatizations, lax tax collection, deviating state funds) in exchange for securing the long-term stability, prosperity and security of the country, without which their own and their children's social positions and rights (including with regard to their property) would not be guaranteed.

To win over the armed forces, the President may have to offer them 'sweeteners', i.e. more sophisticated weaponry enabling them successfully to intervene in conflicts which eventually may threaten the country's security. However, with patriotism among the military certainly not less developed than among the population at large, they also may be attracted by the idea of contributing to the civilian tasks of modernizing Russia, e.g. public works performed by soldiers.

The benign President would be ready to accept the present borders of Russia and the CIS. However, he would insist on them not isolating Russia but remaining open. Therefore, he would strive for more profound integration and a more pronounced role for Russia in the presently loose union of the Commonwealth. In this, he would move ahead prudently in order not to alienate some of the more reluctant CIS republics or raise suspicions of Russia wanting to fully dominate them again and, thus, risk losing them for ever. Effectively, he is opposed to full domination as a result of his democratic convictions but also because of the heavy economic burden involved for Russia. However, he would look for a CIS military alliance (even more so if NATO were to expand eastwards without strengthening partnership with Russia at the same time) and press for a Russian peace-keeping role if his later proposals for a pan-European security arrangement should fail (once more because the West may not be willing to join peace-keeping operations and who else but Russia should do it then?).

Rebuilding Russian power and influence via a thorough modernization of the country (instead of re-strengthening it militarily) would meet strong braking forces

Firstly, in Russia's history the modernizers have always been defeated in the end by those wanting to build 'Great Russia' on the basis of its military power. Modernizing Russia requires a long-term effort during which it would be weak and vulnerable. This would only be acceptable if the élites perceived Russia's vulnerability as not being exploited. The stance of Western policy, as well as developments in China, therefore, is of utmost importance for such a scenario to materialize. Western security policy would have to avoid giving the impression of wanting to isolate, contain and encircle Russia. Furthermore, the West would have to leave no doubt about its readiness to admit Russia to its cultural and economic zone.

However, the *benign authoritarian scenario* has every potential to strongly irritate the West and cause negative reactions:

- *The President's move towards a guided democracy may be interpreted as a step back to strongly authoritarian rule.* However, in the near future, the present political system may prove to be even more authoritarian if presidential elections were manipulated. The West would have to decide whether it attaches more importance to a system resembling Western models on paper or one responding better to Russia's traditions and the needs of its current situation.

94

- *The benign President may have to become rather malign and purge the State apparatus* from all sorts of 'corrupt and criminal elements' since without a loyal apparatus much of his reform legislation would remain on paper only and he could not successfully attack the Mafia. He may use all sorts of methods except legally defensible ones (measured by Western standards) since these are not yet at his disposal. Russia has not yet a rule of law with a reliable police and judiciary.
- Furthermore, *Western politicians may perceive the President's CIS-integration agenda as an attempt to somehow rebuild the empire.*
- *The West may therefore find it difficult to believe in the good intentions of the President.* It may react by slowing down economic cooperation and assistance and isolating Russia politically or in the field of military security. This clearly would play into the hands of the anti-Western forces in Russia and those wanting to build Russian 'greatness' on military force.

Secondly, Russia may not (yet) be ready for the President's long-term policy agenda. Whether it could be carried through is uncertain and, therefore, many of the élites and business people may prefer to care for their present and future personal security on an individual basis, i.e. by fast personal enrichment, at a time when unclear legislation and administrative procedures, corruption and 'wild capitalism' prevail.

Thirdly, it is uncertain whether such a Chinese-type model combining strong political leadership with rather far-reaching economic liberalism would produce quick results in Russia. Compared to China, Russia is already highly industrialized (though with a strong bias to military goods); its cultural traditions may be less favourable to economic activity; its immense natural resources encourage business people to strive more for economic rents (from exploiting these resources) than producing (consumer) goods. However, without quick success, the benign President may rapidly lose the support and faith of the population.

Fourthly, such a benign authoritarian President would need to be very charismatic to win over the support of the population. For the moment, however, no such personality has appeared on Russia's political landscape. Yeltsin was considered to be such a person; however, nowadays, most would perceive him as a muddling-through President.

2.3.3. Malign authoritarianism

The scenario of a malign authoritarian President

> *The President is driven by the desire to stop the present turmoil and make Russia 'respected again' as a 'Great Power'.*

However, he does not go back to Communism since it did not prove to be appropriate for a modern economy. Moreover, such a return is not in the interests of the country's old and new élites (which he could override only by the use of brutal force); nor would it convince the people of a 'bright future', and thus contribute to the cohesion of society. Instead, the President would adopt a nationalistic or even chauvinist agenda.

The President recentralizes power around him; he also effectively subordinates the regional leaders to his rule and bases his actions on the established power structures. There is no immediate resistance to his authoritarian leadership.

Law and order rank high on his agenda. Order may appear but the rule of law is not respected; the judiciary might even be brutally misused. The Mafia is attacked primarily in order to remove competing power structures.

He controls the mass media and uses it as a propaganda tool. The Duma is marginalized and manipulated. Civil society is increasingly dominated by nationalist ideology. There is a general atmosphere of fear and an increasingly strong police state.

The President effectively subordinates the armed forces and enforcement agencies to his command.

They are loyal and even blindly obedient to him, in both internal and external conflicts.

The President continues with economic reforms but tends to implement strongly interventionist policies.

He reforms the tax system with a preference for 'taxing the rich' and enforces tax collection. He invests in the welfare and health system, but also in the modernization of the army's equipment and the maintenance of Russia's research potential (i.e. development of modern weaponry).

However, he cannot fully control the flight of capital and can count even less on its return. Thus, national investment would remain low and foreign investment would dry up. The economy would end up in stagnation, at best. Russia would be strongly protectionist and put pressure on the other CIS members to follow suit.

With his rhetoric and actions the President contributes to ungrounded national and ethnic confidence.

This may contribute to national solidarity, but at the price of ethnic intolerance. The latter may feed fundamentalist Islamic tendencies and conflicts in the south. He frightens the Baltic states. Society becomes more brutal and Russian minorities in the 'near abroad' receive the most attention.

On the international stage, the President behaves as the leader of an assertive Great Power.

He attempts to enlarge the Russian power base by effectively controlling the CIS and he undertakes a number of unilateral actions on some international issues (former Yugoslavia, disarmament, etc.) to remind the West that Russia is a 'Great Power'. However, he is aware of Russia's present weakness and this restrains his assertiveness.

Driving forces

In this scenario psychological elements are a major driving force; that is, actual despair, hurt pride and feelings of national humiliation. Perceptions of Russia becoming marginalized in world affairs and its security eventually being threatened may add to this.

For ordinary Russians, feelings of national and personal humiliation may originate mostly in the daily chaos, rampant crime, drastically falling living standards, decaying health care and strongly reduced life-expectancy, all of which results in demoralization and deep personal insecurity (best reflected in very low birth rates). Much of this is attributed to Russia trying to adapt to Western economic and social models, ignoring its own special character. Among the intelligentsia (living largely on meagre government budgets) there is also strong discontent, not least since they lost their formerly rather privileged position and now find themselves at the lower end of the social and wealth hierarchy. This loss of status, combined with their disgust at 'rampant capitalism' and the new business class, which is perceived as having no 'class' at all, but also the excessive intrusion of Hollywood and the pop-culture into Russia, have strongly reduced the intelligentsia's traditional admiration of the West.

So, the natural allies of the West have nearly been forced into silence: the intelligentsia, too, is looking for national appeal.

Lost pride

The loss of the status of a superpower may be acceptable rationally since it overburdened the Russian economy; however, psychologically, it hurts the pride of even ordinary Russians. Even more difficult for them to digest is the loss of the empire with its common cultural and economic space, and Russia's shrinking to its size of 200 years ago at the time of Peter the Great, with its present borders delineated rather artificially by the Bolshevik commissars of the 1920s and the 1930s. To many Russians these borders inspire unease, especially to those living in these areas, and so does the fact that 25 million of their compatriots now live outside Russia in politically unstable countries, with their mother tongue mostly not accepted as an official language. Admittedly, such feelings are not dominant at the moment. However, political propaganda could strengthen them, and especially so when insinuating that economic misery is a result of the loss of empire.

Reasons for anti-Western sentiment

Perceptions of the West being highly satisfied with the dwarfing of Russia, of it opposing any form of reintegration and denying Russia special rights to somehow control the post-Soviet space and thus to pursue its 'legitimate' security interests, further add to feelings of defeat and humiliation, and to anti-Western attitudes, mostly so among parts of the élites. Furthermore, there are suspicions that the West wants to overrun Russia economically, of it only being interested in Russia's natural resources, ignoring Russian cultural and scientific achievements and barring it from gaining access to the world market for high technology.

Russian élites also are suspicious of the West's (i.e. the US's) strong interest in Central Asia and the Caucasus where rich energy resources are considered by US politicians to be the next century's energy supply alternative to the Persian Gulf. They perceive Turkey and Iran, and also China, as wanting to extend their influence to this region. So there are suspicions of different players trying to play their own game in a region which

99

Russians consider their own backyard, eventually adding fuel to all sorts of potential conflicts (such as those stemming from the cultural and religious dividing line between the Orthodox Church and Islam) which could, indeed, threaten Russia's security. Obviously, such perceptions and suspicions nourish anti-Western and nationalistic sentiments, as do the patronizing attitudes of Westerners, deception about meagre Western 'assistance' and, at the same time, shame about Russia's needing or accepting assistance at all.

There is, then, strong potential for Russia to retreat into isolation based on anti-Western sentiment, even more so as suspicion of the West (as it has been persistently taught over hundreds of years) is inherent to the thinking of ordinary Russians. There is no shortage of people advocating the restoration of a military camp atmosphere. They preach in favour of an unquestionable leader who will mobilize national resources, and is in favour of strong discipline. They want Russia to reunify with Slavs in the west and the Caucasus and Muslims in the south; and to develop again into a military 'Great Power' or even 'Superpower'. The methods of 'reintegration' may be quite peaceful, or they may be violent, with the latter becoming more likely as time passes and the non-Russian republics manage somehow to consolidate politically and economically, and develop their own notion of identity which, of course, would build on anti-Russian premises.

As argued earlier, the Communist Party may be able to use the large patriotic potential of the people first, in the forthcoming elections, but rebuilding the empire would have to come along under a new and non-discredited ideological banner; that is, under a national-radical authoritarian one (though this would not be new either, but the banner of the tsars). Thus, any Red-Brown coalition would be a temporary alliance only, with the Brown forces winning power in the end.

Braking forces

Although Russia has proved time and again in its history that the patriotic potential of its people can be mobilized to a point at which no sacrifice is too great, there seem to be strong braking forces.

First, the new, young generation of Russians is very pragmatic. Army duty is not popular. National prestige ranks much lower in importance than individual freedom and the chance to break through to wealth and higher status in society. The young are not a majority of the population, of course, but are the most active economically and politically, and (most importantly) it is they who would have to pay with their lives for aggressive policies. Therefore, some conclude that to persuade young people to fight for the restoration of the empire would be much more difficult today than at any other time in Russian history.

Second, with Afghanistan, Russia, too, has had its Vietnam. The war was highly unpopular and exhausted Russia's resources as well. The civil war in Chechnya lasting much longer than expected, humiliating the Russian Army and revealing its lack of sophisticated weaponry, as well as the Yugoslavian tragedy, may well have increased fears of any aggression resulting in long and drawn-out conflicts. Not only would Russians have to pay a high price in terms of lives, but they would, in the end, experience lower living standards as well.

Third, rebuilding the empire by force would necessarily imply a recentralization of political power in order to allow for the mobilization of all national resources – needed to rebuild, modernize and keep Russia's military machinery running. However, any recentralization of power is just the opposite of what the regional leaders, including the leaders of big companies (except those of the military-industrial complex, of course) have been fighting for since the early Brezhnev years.

101

They have managed to become little tsars and they want to remain that way, especially since it offers them many opportunities for personal enrichment.

Fourth, the new Russian capitalists too could hardly have an interest in rebuilding the empire in an aggressive way, since this would risk ending up in a centrally planned war economy. Ownership of private property could still continue but, of course, a remilitarization of the economy would constitute a great waste of resources; it would outlaw Russia politically and, thus, cut off Russian business from international markets and investments for a long time as well. Although Russian capitalists probably would welcome a new empire or a Russian dominated CIS (but certainly not the perverse one that the USSR was, where the centre paid for the 'colonies'), they also know that this can be achieved in a more civilized way by using their advances in privatization, capital accumulation and intellectual resources to buy up the resources and businesses of other republics, i.e. by dominating them fully in economic terms.

Fifth, the present Constitution invests the Russian President with more power, at least formally, than even Stalin actually held. The élites, apart from extremists, may be extremely reluctant, therefore, to lend support to any candidate who has the personal potential for terrorism and adventurous foreign policy, when attempting to run for election or to grab power in whatever way.

2.3.4. Weak centre

The weak centre scenario

The central power has weakened considerably.

The centre may appear to be strong but actually it is much weaker because the implementation of laws has to be carried out by the regions. Or, it may actually be weak as a result of political stalemate. The already loose federation might further weaken and develop into a confederation. Some regions are tempted to loosen their ties with the Russian Federation and seek independence. Reasons for doing so might be their peripheral location and the economic attractiveness of third (perhaps neighbouring) countries, a wealth of natural resources, ethnic motivations or a sense of neglect by the centre.

Regional military leaders support their civilian counterparts.

They instruct their soldiers who to vote for or lend their strong arm for various purposes. They are encouraged to this sort of cooperation as a result of an undermined and discredited central authority, and a progressive breakdown of centralized military command structures because of the persistent erosion of discipline, endemic corruption, and involvement in criminal activities including illegal arms sales. Thus, the army becomes regionalized with only some forces of cooperation maintained.

The Russian Federation's economic and legal area disintegrates.

The increasing power of the regions results in increasing regional legislation. It disrupts trade flows between regions, and ultimately results in economic collapse and destitution that is in itself a self-accelerating deterioration.

An acutely fragmented society emerges.

Rampant crime, brutality and breakdown of law become part of the Russians' daily lives. Anti-semitism, racism and various '-isms' are common. The high level of dissatisfaction makes people susceptible to demagogy and behave as if they had nothing to lose.

Russia is fully preoccupied with itself, inward-looking, self-isolating.

103

Driving forces

In this scenario the major driving forces are the ethnically motivated desire for independence, expectations of regional economic advantages as a result of more pronounced decentralization, and, more fundamentally, the regional leaders' interest in consolidating their power and gaining control of economic resources and the proceeds from their eventual privatization. The different centrifugal forces may combine, depending on the circumstances, but could result in attempts to split off from the Russian Federation only in the case of a peripherally located region, allowing it to re-orient its trade and economy to new partners without having to pass across other Russian territory. Such temptations are strongest in the regions of the Caucasus and north of Mongolia, where there seem to be quite a number of potential 'Chechnyas'.

While the ethnic search for independence is the most dangerous threat, the most massive centrifugal force seems to come from the regional élites' hunger for power, most pronounced in comparatively rich regions and less so in those depending on the finance of the centre.

Prospects for federalism

Nominally, orderly regionalization, i.e. federalization, ranks high on the political agenda, but in reality it seems that the centre, and especially the President, do not want to lose their grip on the regions for reasons of power, but of course also for financial reasons as in the case of regions rich in natural resources.

One should expect the centrifugal forces working towards spontaneous regionalization to re-strengthen as soon as the centre shows any signs of weakness. For this to happen, there are a number of possibilities: several Chechnyas might emerge at once, absorbing the centre's energy; the centre might become paralysed again as a result of new infighting for power, eventually resulting even in a civil war between 'Reds' and 'Whites'; or it may be paralysed by corruption.

Barring extremes, there seem to be strong braking forces acting against disintegration and the eventual splitting-up of Russia

First, disintegration would not be in anyone's interest, except for some extremist regional leaders. Therefore, a consensus among all sorts of political and economic groupings may emerge rather rapidly about saving Russian 'motherlands'. After all, over 80 per cent of the population are Russians, and though there are over a hundred ethnic groupings, they are usually a minority even if the republics/regions are named after them.

Second, the regional leaders certainly want more power (especially economic), but probably not at the price of Russia's disintegration. Rather, they would grab it in order to have a bargaining chip for (later) negotiations with the centre about Russia's regionalization and federalization. They are patriotic and responsible too and proved it when, after the abolition of the Party and the Plan, they used their old boys' networks to organize inter-regional barter deals (wheat for steel, for example) – certainly not to their personal disadvantage – thus preventing a complete collapse of Russia's economy.

Third, the (increasing) attempts to somehow strengthen the CIS would reduce the most independent-minded Caucasian regions' options: they could become formally independent (and remain poor) or (re-)integrate with Russia. But they could not become really independent, that is, economically viable states (if this ever was an option) since all of their neighbours would follow Russia's rules. They would be encircled and this seems to be one more factor behind Russia's plans to make the CIS an effective organization, or somehow rebuild the empire.

As a result, it seems that the weak centre scenario is only a short-term possibility, except in case of civil war.

2.3.5.   Gradual democratization

The scenario of gradual democratization

> *Extremist forces are marginalized in the election process and stable political parties emerge.*

The Constitution is amended to establish genuine checks and balances on the President's power. The centre and the regions agree on new constitutional rules (a new Federation Treaty). Freedom of the press is allowed. Utmost attention is given to excluding the Mafia from the political and judicial decision-making process.

> *The armed forces and enforcement agencies are loyal to the Constitution.*

They are under civil control and accept the primacy of politics. They refuse to be drawn into internal conflicts and are reluctant to resort to military solutions in the 'near abroad' and beyond.

A clear economic policy agenda emerges only slowly.

Reforms could be partly rolled back, especially those which hurt the population most visibly, such as the privatization of housing. For progress in other areas, there may be insufficient common political will or too strong an influence of vested interests.

Although the Government aims at establishing a rule of law, the Mafia becomes even more influential, since the Government hesitates or lacks the power to act strongly against it. The Government/Parliament attempts to create the legal and institutional framework for a market economy and to enforce the rules. However, it is reluctant to cut subsidies, for fear of unemployment, and all too willing to pay for social welfare. Both reduce the scope for investment and economic growth.

A moderate national consolidation becomes possible.

It is based on the spreading of human values and freedom, and eventually confidence grows in the new generation of politicians. The Government exerts a positive and stabilizing influence on neighbouring states and adopts a benevolent attitude towards strengthening the CIS. That is to say, Russia is reluctant to take advantage of its *de facto* dominance, but economic reintegration clearly remains a goal.

A gradually democratized Russia wants to be a positive and full partner in world institutions.

External relations follow the pattern described in the benign authoritarianism scenario, but with economic integration taking much more time.

Driving forces

In this scenario the major driving forces are the high level of general education, the success of *glasnost* and Russia's opening-up to the West. Russians no longer discuss politics only with close friends around the kitchen table but voice disagreements in public. There is a free press with some courageous and excellent journalists, though for lack of funds coverage is available in the big cities only, and there are free and critical radio and television channels, though not all of them broadcast nation-wide. There are personal contacts with Westerners, albeit mostly limited to the various élites in the big cities, and there is an increasing number of people travelling to the West or even getting an education there. Russia is open to the flow of information from the West. Therefore, and despite the reservations made, the values of individual freedom, human rights and democracy may gradually spread – in the big cities first and in the provinces later.

Braking forces

There seem to be strong braking forces against Russia's development into a parliamentary democracy (including judicial checks and balances) in the foreseeable future.

First, it is questionable whether a majority, or important groupings, of the political, bureaucratic and economic élites are democratically minded. They certainly do not want to go back to a totalitarian regime and, therefore, many are highly critical of the present Constitution with its overwhelming concentration of power in the hands of the President. However, whether they accept the people as ultimately sovereign is still another question. The distance between the élites and the masses seems to be huge and attitudes of paternalism or even disdain are rather strong. The élites may prefer an oligarchic system or a guided democracy with some sort of parliament composed of members of the élites. Even many democratic-minded members of the élite seem to favour a Russian model of democracy, however that may be defined. They fear large swings in the popular mood, and others may think that it fits much better with Russian traditions, i.e. habits of negotiating compromises behind closed doors (which must not be in contradiction to the bitter fighting in public).

Second, it is questionable whether the population at large already is or will become sufficiently mature to handle parliamentary democracy in the foreseeable future. Their voting for the Communists and the Zhirinovskyites raises doubts about this, since some of these politicians hardly disguise their contempt for democracy and would abandon an electoral system once in power. On the other hand, it is the people's only possibility to express their strong disapproval of reforms which benefit only a few and greatly harm the overwhelming majority, up to now at least. Still, protest-voting on the scale of the parliamentary elections of December 1995 justifies scepticism.

Third, there is widespread apathy, passivity and alienation from political life among the population. It never had the opportunity to actively participate in democracy and, therefore, the predominant feeling seems to be that an individual person does not count and cannot influence much at all. It is a feeling of individual impotence ('We are only little people'). In addition, alienation between politicians and the population seems to be a self-feeding process; the population considers them greedy, ambitious people, interested only in their personal career, not trustworthy, and the politicians do everything to justify such prejudice. For example, in regional and local elections administrators of all sorts used their positions to win a seat in Parliament. They now control (and enrich themselves), which cannot inspire respect for democracy. As a result, there are arguments such as: why do we need a Parliament or pluralism? One good leader (which seems to mean a strong leader) would be sufficient. And these are not limited to regional/local elections but apply even more to the presidential ones.

Fourth, Soviet Russia never knew a civil society through whose institutions people could openly discuss, learn to compromise and jointly to defend their interests. They were all Party-dominated or spied upon and, therefore, people have learned to mistrust such institutions. In addition, today's daily struggle for personal survival leaves people little time for building and engaging in the networks of an emerging civil society. Without such networks, however, it may be difficult for democracy to take root.

Fifth, the political party system still awaits consolidation. The only party with a large membership (some 500,000 to 600,000) and strong organization is that of the Communists (plus its sister organization the Agrarian Party) and Zhirinovsky's Liberal

Democrats, whereas the democrats are still split. Of course, this may change, but developing clear party profiles, organizations and attracting members will take much time, even more so for an opposition party and in a society not used to active participation in political life.

Sixth, a broad middle class and bourgeoisie that could become a stabilizer of democracy has not yet emerged. There are 3 to 5 per cent 'rich' people (earning between 60,000 and 120,000 US dollars or more a year) and, altogether, 10 to 12 per cent (according to Gorbachev) who have profited from reforms. The huge 'rest' is worse off than before and it may take many years for their living-standards merely to recover to the previous level.

Seventh, it seems to be true that, apart from some journalists, the liberal intelligentsia who were at the forefront of the *glasnost* era, carry less weight today than ever. So an important multiplier for the propagation of human rights and democracy has become weak.

Finally, democratic values may gradually spread in the big cities but less in the provinces, as long as many of the latter are ruled like personal fiefdoms by governors (imposed from the centre) or authoritarian regional bosses. Therefore, federalization would be important for the gradual democratization of the country as a whole. However, the élites in power in the centre, and not only the actual President, may not want to loosen the centre's ties with the regions, for fear of unleashing centrifugal forces, or losing powerful allies in case new power struggles in the centre emerge.

2.4. WHICH SCENARIOS ARE RELEVANT FOR THE YEAR 2000 AND BEYOND?

The above scenarios present fairly clear-cut alternative paths for the future and help identify the driving and braking forces. In reality, of course, there are no clear-cut alternatives, but a continuous lurching back and forth. Different scenarios will prevail for some time only to be dominated again by others. The configuration at a specific moment depends on the dynamics and relative strength of the driving and braking forces at play. These are, however, impossible to assess accurately, especially during periods of revolutionary change. Our scenarios also have different time spans: some have the potential to materialize now, some later, and some again would only materialize as a result of another specific scenario. In addition, some scenarios are sustainable over time, while others are more ephemeral.

Therefore, it is necessary to specify the *time span* envisaged and to select the scenarios which are *relevant* in each case.

2.4.1. Past experience of reforms

The fact that important elements of all the scenarios presented have already materialized over the last four years serves to underline their relevance. Due to the turbulence of the period, they overlap, however. President Yeltsin showed benign authoritarian features when implementing his far-reaching economic reform agenda, which he could do without meeting much resistance from the country's élites who were paralysed by the implosion of the Soviet empire. The paralysis gave way to the re-emergence of strong vested interests, blocking economic reform, and subsequently resulted in muddling-through policies. Throughout the same period, we saw a gradual democratization: democratic values spread and freedom of the press was achieved. In parallel to this development, the weak centre scenario emerged which was finally stopped in a malign authoritarian way, by the bombardment of the Congress of People's Deputies. The President's fight with the Congress was not principally about reforms, or at what speed they should take place, but about who should have the ultimate power in Russia: the former party-oligarchy (including the regional bosses) or the President. With the adoption of the Constitution the question of power was settled and since then we have seen muddling-through policies. They probably fit the best with the interests of many of the people surrounding the President. They also fit best his own personal interest, which is to consolidate presidential power by avoiding major clashes of interest and to follow a deliberate policy of 'divide and rule'.

2.4.2. Russia by the year 2000

If President Yeltsin were to be replaced, Russia could enter a new period of turbulence. Elections could be cancelled or the present Kremlin *kamarilla* could refuse to hand over power to an elected successor. This would be the moment when the armed forces and enforcement agencies would have to declare or demonstrate whether they are loyal to the Constitution or to the *kamarilla*. Barring such extreme developments, which other scenarios are relevant?

Benign authoritarianism

There is no personality on the present political stage conducive to the realization of this scenario. Neither is it likely that Russia's capitalists and regional leaders would be ready to lend support to a sort of 'Pinochet' agenda which would imply the acceptance of some reduction of their power.[3]

Muddling through

As indicated earlier, the present tendencies favour a continuation of muddling-through policies. If President Yeltsin were to be replaced, one should expect Russia's private and state-owned media to join forces in order to support a 'muddling-through' candidate.[4]

Malign authoritarianism

If personalities such as Lebed or Zyuganov came to power, it could be that they would turn against the Mafia. Tough policies towards Russia's capitalists, however, would risk entailing capital flight and economic deterioration, leading them to change course and embark on economic muddling-through policies again, especially as they could not count on a fully loyal state apparatus. The more aggressive features of this scenario, notably an aggression towards the 'near abroad', seem unlikely. Lebed may not want to pursue such policies, and Zyuganov would not be able to mobilize the population at large and even less the younger generations, possibly not even the army. However, a malign authoritarian leader may increase political, economic and psychological pressure on other CIS republics to integrate at least militarily with Russia.

Weak centre

This scenario could well happen parallel to muddling-through policies, and would be a definite possibility if any handing-over of power at the centre resulted in (temporary) political paralysis.

Gradual democratization

A Western model of democracy is not possible. Although democratic values may continue to spread and the number of democrats may increase (for instance, if a benign regime scenario were to materialize and a marked increase in the population's living standards were achieved), there is huge potential for a further discrediting of democracy (for instance, in the case of protracted conflicts of power in the centre or continued policy-making by muddling through).

2.4.3. Russia beyond the year 2000

Which scenario materializes in the next four years will have a crucial effect on development beyond the year 2000.

The benign authoritarian scenario could be continued

Later, as further generations will have grown up in a rather liberal and democratic environment (and convinced or nostalgic Communists will have disappeared) and when the benefits of the process of transformation will also have reached the population at large, a benign authoritarian regime could be followed by the gradual democratization scenario.

The muddling-through scenario could continue for a while

This seems likely only if it were underpinned by an increasingly tougher authoritarian rule, since the population would not vote for such policies. A refusal by the new/old establishment to hand over power to a democratically elected successor to President Yeltsin would only anticipate this scenario's authoritarian component.

The malign authoritarian scenario is a possibility

This scenario could follow on from the muddling-through regime. A malign authoritarian may not stand much chance of being voted into power, but social explosions or a military *coup* could somehow put him into office. However, in order for this scenario to materialize, the decisive development would have to take place before too many young people (potential soldiers) have adjusted to the capitalist environment and, hence, have become more interested in jobs and social status than in national glory.

The weak centre scenario could emerge gradually

It may be the result of ethnic tensions getting out of control or a malign authoritarian leader's aggressive policies towards the 'near abroad', leading to drawn-out conflicts and a weakening of the country. However, it is clearly not a sustainable scenario, but one which might invite a 'strong' leader to seize power in order to rebuild Russia.

2.4.4. Conclusions

Russia still has the opportunity to continue the reform process which, in fact, began at the turn of the century but was interrupted and brought to a halt by World War I and the October Revolution. At present, the country knows neither a pluralist democracy nor a market economy governed by clear rules and competition. However, since 1992, Russia has moved in the direction of modernization and has made more progress than ever before in Russian history. Even if Russia does not yet know a true civil society, personal initiative and responsibility are spreading and people have become increasingly individualistic and critical towards all sorts of ideologies. Anti-totalitarian attitudes have become strong, but commitment to democratic values is still weak. Daily chaos and economic misery may not be conducive to the emergence of such a commitment. However, to conclude from this that Russians are not yet mature enough to take on the responsibility of democracy and, therefore, need authoritarian leadership, would be dangerous.

In fact, it seems as though not too much freedom has been granted to the people, but too little. There is still an almighty and patronizing bureaucracy paralysing personal initiative and preventing the emergence of clear rules and a rule of law, and thus rendering people helpless. The Kremlin bureaucracy, regional leaders and some economic groups have united (again) in a cartel of power kept going by bribery and corruption and by furthering its own interests, regardless of the population. The real threat to Russian democracy is coming from this cartel. It could well decide to force an open or hidden authoritarian regime into power in order to preserve its privileged position, contributing further to the feeling of helplessness among the population, and thereby put a real hurdle in the way of the emergence of democratic attitudes. Internal political and social dynamics will be the most important elements deciding Russia's orientations toward its 'near abroad' and the rest of the outside world. The West will need to remain vigilant and firm in its attitudes towards Russia. It should not deceive itself by believing that Russia is becoming democratic when the tendency is towards a more authoritarian regime. Neither should it be concentrating solely on the Kremlin at a moment when the latter's power is increasingly challenged by other political (the regions) and social (the new capitalists) forces. Rather, it should strive to establish contacts with responsible forces of all sorts which could act as a kind of lobby to persuade Russia to keep up a reasonable relationship with the West. Furthermore, the West should avoid exploiting the continued Russian weakness. It is clear that Russia will not remain weak forever, but Western people who think so and act accordingly may play into the hands of those who want to rebuild Russia's power on military strength rather than on a modernized economy and society.

Notes

1 This paper was finalized in May 1996. It remains valid.
2 The methodology used for building the different scenarios was the common matrix-approach which consists of: (1) defining the relevant key variables, (2) elaborating as precisely as possible the different constellations they may take, which means to ask what exactly is imaginable (and why), and (3) linking the different constellations of one key variable with all the constellations of each

of the other key variables by (numerically, on a scale of 1 to 5, for example) assessing the strength of these links. The assessments were made with the assistance of Russian experts. From these numerical assessments the computer calculates which constellations of each of the key variables fit best and, thus, represent a consistent scenario. Scenarios obtained this way can be submitted to experts to judge whether they are likely to materialize, which is usually done by applying the Delphi-method. However, we thought that when asking experts, it was likely that they would give answers too strongly influenced by on-going events. Their choice for one or another scenario would not have revealed the motivation behind their choice. Therefore, we decided to explicitly list the driving and braking forces for the different scenarios and to invite the reader to add or delete such forces with the passing of time. Attentive observation of these forces should help to identify the emergence of new power configurations pushing toward another scenario. Needless to say, there is no method for 'dynamising' the static scenarios presented and developing a 'sequencing' of scenarios.

3 President Yeltsin does not seem to possess any longer the physical force to override the resistance stemming from various quarters. If he were to to be replaced, the personalities with the ability to play a 'benign' authoritarian role seem to stand little chance of being elected President.

4 A recent analysis of the Russian media reveals that their present favourite seems to be Moscow's mayor, Mr Lushkov. General Lebed, on the other hand, attracts little attention and even less sympathy.

Chapter 3

Ukraine: balancing between East and West

3.1. INTRODUCTION

This chapter looks at the most important players and factors in the Ukraine and those important for relations with Russia. However, and unlike the chapter on Russia, it will start with the shaping factors since, as in most of the non-Russian republics, these seem to be even more important than the different players, or at least to limit severely their scope of action.

3.2. EXTERNAL FACTORS

Russia will remain the most important external factor shaping Ukraine's development, for geopolitical, security, economic and historical reasons.

Geography dictates continued Russian interest in Ukraine. With Belarus, Ukraine now separates Russia from central Europe; it makes Russian power in Europe more remote, and could contribute to changing Russian self-perceptions by highlighting its 'Eurasian' identity. However, Russia does not seem to want to be 'shifted' east but would prefer to remain an important European player. Especially because, as a former superpower and a still influential regional power, Russia retains direct interests in south-eastern Europe (e.g. with the Balkans and Moldova/Trans-Dnestria) which can be most easily accessed via Ukraine. Russian gas exports to Western Europe transit through Ukraine, and Russia retains an interest in the strategically important ports of the Black Sea, which give both countries access to the Mediterranean and hence to the wider Europe beyond. Russia, therefore, will want its interests to be taken into consideration in Kiev. Also, Ukraine borders other new, independent states (Georgia, Moldova, Belarus), some with unresolved internal conflicts, as yet unspecified national interests and unstable political systems. In all of these regions Russia wants to, and indeed will, play an important role.

Russia will essentially decide Ukraine's security: whether the direction Russia takes is positive or negative will depend exclusively on its internal development. The West will hardly be willing to counter-balance Russia's influence or instability. Even in the best case scenario of gradual democratization and integration into the Western world's institutions, Russia would still have psychological problems, to say the least, in accepting that an integral part of the Russian 'motherland', to which the Ukraine is perceived to belong, could join NATO, Russia's number one enemy for 40 years. In the event of a less favourable internal evolution, Russia might find it unacceptable for the Ukraine to serve as a buffer-zone between itself and the West and would want to reintegrate it into Russian-dominated, i.e. CIS, security structures.

Soviet Russia had made the Ukrainian economy an integral part of the Soviet economic system, with deliberate heavy dependence on imports from and exports to Russia and other CIS countries. Ukraine can hardly produce anything of its own, but needs Russian/CIS product components or Russian assembly lines for final products. For gas and oil, it is completely dependent on Russian supplies. Ukraine has neither the money nor the know-how to restructure and modernize its industry swiftly and re-orient its trade to the West, nor could it pay for new pipelines to substitute Russian energy supplies, or for investments to save energy. For the foreseeable future, therefore, the Ukraine will remain strongly dependent on the CIS and notably Russian markets and energy supplies. So, to improve its economic situation, Ukraine will have no other choice but to reintegrate into the CIS with a view to improving its economic situation, while at the same time developing economic links with other regions.

With Russia now asking near to world market prices for energy, Ukraine's import bill has increased. To pay for it, it would have to increase its export prices which, however, is made harder by the very fact that high energy prices have made many of its traditional energy-intensive export products less competitive in comparison with Russian ones. Therefore, one might expect persistent balance-of-payment problems, adding to its existing five billion US dollar foreign debt to Russia. Russia might 'assist' Ukraine in exchanging debt for equity or energy for property rights (e.g. pipelines carrying Russian gas to the West) which, together with Russian private capital flows, would result in an increasing economic influence, comparable to that of the US in Canada.

History links Ukraine closely to Russia, though it is, of course, a myth that the Ukraine was in Russian possession for nearly three and a half centuries, making many believe that it was only a matter of time before it would 'return home'. In fact, only a small part of Ukraine ('Little Russia') belonged to the Russian empire for so long. However, history has left Ukraine with a Russian minority of 11.5 million which makes up 22 per cent of the population. Russia is clearly concerned about the welfare of its compatriots and not would accept discrimination against them.

The West is the second most important external shaping factor, but of course of a very different nature to Russia. It has no real self-interest as to the future of the Ukraine, except in matters of defence, such as not having another (unstable) nuclear power, unsafe nuclear power plants, or social upheavals with potential spill-over effects to Europe. The West wishes to preserve Ukraine's independence in order to firmly establish a buffer zone between it and an unpredictable Russia.

However, the Western-minded Ukrainians seem to perceive the West differently, as a pole of attraction. For them, joining the West is tantamount to escaping the embrace of the eternally 'backward Russia' (though, for the moment, it is the Ukraine which is more backward). Independent Ukraine's first govern-ment (President Kravchuk) had hoped for close ties with the European Union and even for Western security guarantees against Russia, in exchange for renouncing nuclear weapons. The present government (President Kuchma) has understood that such a barter trade is unrealistic and that security is always relative, with some having more and others less, depending on their geographical situation and exposure to threats. Ukrainians could eventually learn to live with this, but the West could disturb such a process by admitting some Central and Eastern European countries into NATO while keeping others out. The fact that the Ukraine would almost certainly be kept out, at least for the foreseeable future, is likely to be perceived by Ukrainians as a clear signal that it was being pushed back by the West into the Russian orbit. Such a decision could do more harm to the country than Western assistance might ever make up for. It would encourage Russia to consolidate its own sphere of security to which Ukraine is perceived to belong, and to exert corresponding pressure.

3.3. INTERNAL FACTORS

The most important internal shaping factor is Ukraine's ethno-cultural division. Ukraine means 'borderland, periphery', and in fact comprises the borderlands of former empires, often hostile towards each other: the Polish-Lithuanian, Ottoman, Austro-Hungarian and Russian empires, and Romania. All of them have left their marks and the Ukraine nowadays can be considered as a bipolar country, with an eastern and a western pole with Kiev at the centre playing a mediating role in the struggle between the two. The two poles differ from each other in terms of ethnic origin and language (large presence of ethnic Russians and predominance of the Russian language in the east/ predominance of Ukrainians and the Ukrainian language in the west), religion (Orthodoxy/Catholicism), social and cultural tradition (collectivism and state paternalism in the east/ individualism in the west), economic orientation (state ownership/private property), geopolitical orientation (towards Russia and Eurasia/towards the West or Europe) and historical perceptions (feeling part of Russia/oppressed by Russia).[1]

The Ukraine's 91 per cent vote for independence in 1991 helped it forget about its ethno-cultural divide, whereas the elections in 1994 highlighted it again. Eastern Ukraine voted for anti-reform-minded political forces on the left and closer ties with the CIS, while Western Ukraine preferred pro-reform national-democratic or national-radical forces and orientations to the West. Many feared that the country would split, with Eastern Ukraine seeking to join Russia. However, President Kuchma is an Easterner and, while working for closer cooperation with Russia, he also became a staunch defender of Ukraine's territorial integrity and independence.

3.3.1.   The struggle for national cohesion

The question remains how to keep this country together permanently, and how and on what to build a national identity as a force of social cohesion since ethnicity, a common history, culture and language cannot serve as a basis. Some claim that it could be built on the bloody historical experiences of the century (wars and civil wars, famine, Stalinist terrorism, etc.) which have persuaded the Ukrainians that they would be more secure if they had greater control over their own affairs, i.e. if

123

they had their own state. To struggle jointly for political democracy could also become a basis for national identity and cohesion. However, this will take time and the risk of a split is great as the state remains very young. The official view is that Ukrainian identity is linked to its territory, an argument which is not convincing, even less so as Ukrainians seem to identify primarily with their region of origin. Assuming that this is the case, it could be concluded that for the ethnic Russians and possibly also for the strongly Russified Ukrainians (native Russian speakers) in the east and south-east, it matters little whether they belong to Ukraine or to Russia, and that their orientation would finally depend on where they believe they would be better off, politically and economically.

Most observers agree that the overwhelming majority in favour of an independent Ukraine was rooted in the illusion that Ukraine was much richer than Russia, and that the latter exploited Ukraine's resources. Similarly, the 1994 election result and the still prevalent support for independence can be explained by the present economic decay which has since dashed hopes of national wealth. Notably, the traditionally rich eastern and south-eastern Ukrainians (in the Donbas region but also in Crimea) feel frustrated because they have subsequently become much poorer, compared with their Russian neighbours. It can be concluded therefore, that the ethno-cultural divide should be seen as a latent risk to the country's cohesion, with the potential to develop into a real threat, if it were combined with economic deception (or other factors, such as ethnic discrimination, carefully avoided so far).

Therefore, some think that the best way to prevent such a threat materializing would be to grant more autonomy to the regions by transforming Ukraine into a federal state. Eastern Ukrainians are strongly in favour of this (notably for the sake of 'reduced regional income redistribution to poor Western Ukraine'), whereas Western Ukrainians oppose federalism out of fear that it could encourage Eastern secessionist tendencies.

President Kuchma is opposed too, fearing disintegration, and is therefore promoting the need for centralized decision-making and a strong presidency.

The regeneration of the economy is essential for the consolidation of the Ukraine's independence. Continued economic misery would further political radicalization and regional antagonisms. It would make the Ukraine vulnerable to Russian pressure and eventually encourage secessionism of Eastern Ukraine and Crimea. Regeneration has to build mainly on closer economic ties with Russia and for this, Ukraine will have to catch up, especially as regards economic reforms. Even more strenuous reform efforts will be required in order to develop economic links with the West.

At the end of 1994, Ukraine had adopted IMF-inspired 'shock-therapy' but whether it can be sustained is not yet clear. It will affect the Ukraine's regions very differently and, therefore, may produce significant tensions, with a direct implication on Ukraine's external orientation. In the case of a tough privatization process[2] the heavily industrialized eastern, Russophile regions would be hit first and hardest, axing up to 40 per cent of the existing jobs. This would almost certainly further strengthen these regions' anti-reformist attitudes and orientation towards Russia.[3] Tensions could further increase if reforms attracted direct foreign investments mostly to the 'green-field sites' in Western Ukraine, as seems likely, rather than to the ecologically devastated Eastern Ukraine. This would encourage calls for greater openness to the West in the western regions, while the recessionist East might, in that case, want to look for help from Russia. Given Ukraine's administrative backwardness, its limited ability to manage regional aid programmes, its still uncertain identity and divided allegiances, such internal tensions could prove difficult to manage. However, sitting on the fence is no alternative either.

Furthermore, most observers agree that shock-therapy will need to be accompanied by substantial foreign assistance in the longer term. However, it is questionable whether the West, whose commitments so far have been grudging and limited, will or can subsidize 52 million Ukrainians over a prolonged period. Russia might be more willing to assist, despite its present leadership's concerns about endangering its own reform prospects by subsidizing other republics. However, Ukraine would most likely have to pay a political price for it.

3.4. MAIN PLAYERS

Ukraine's institutions are still weak and in a state of flux. It has not yet adopted a post-communist constitution since the Presidency and Parliament cannot agree on a proper division of power nor on who controls the government. The still predominantly shared goal of maintaining the country's independence, and the awareness that this requires a government able to act and, especially, to go ahead with economic reforms neglected so far, works in favour of compromises on both sides. Some political and economic successes for the President could tip the balance of power in his favour. Without such success one could not rule out severe confrontation with Parliament in which the left-wing, reform-hostile block accounts for more than 40 per cent of the seats. However, Ukrainians exclude a violent confrontation as happened in Russia in October 1993, because of their 'greater tolerance and realism'.

For the time being, the President rules by decree and the Ministers are directly subordinated to him. He has also managed to subordinate all the democratically elected regional and local governments to his authority. However, he was sensible enough to sweeten their subordination by creating a Council of the Regions as a consultative body since he needs these leaders as allies for his plan to consolidate the presidency as the chief executive organ. The Constition having been amended by presidential decree, the President seems to be in a strong position *de facto*, for the time being.[4]

As in Russia, politics are highly personalized with President Kuchma delegating very little to a small group of close associates or to a small 'Politburo'. This makes for an overcharged agenda and slow decision-making. Within the Parliament too, power is personalized in President Moroz and a handful of deputies. Kuchma is said to have an inclination towards Chile- or Argentina-style reforms, imposed from the top, and Moroz, too, seems to favour 'strong rule' if he ever became president.

Neither the Presidency nor the Parliament see any interest in sharing their still unclear relative powers with a strong judiciary – one that simply provides 'favourable interpretations' of the law is considered to be quite satisfactory. The existing judiciary is rudimentary, badly staffed and does not have the moral stature nor recognized mandate to act with any real authority.

Ukraine's administration was part of the broader Soviet complex, performing within its division of labour. The administrative élite has yet to become accustomed to working together without guidance from Moscow. The central state apparatus is very small in staff numbers (some 12,000), hardly enough to run a large country and to control its regions.

Corruption of state officials is rife, and though fighting it is high on the President's agenda, decisive action hardly seems possible due to the present legal nebulism and the inadequate judiciary. However, corruption and Mafia structures and influences seem far less important than in Russia.

The regions' *de facto* seizure of power was made easier by the long period of reform deadlock in Kiev. The regional political leaders, along with the old *nomenklatura* in Kiev, have 'spontaneously' and illegally privatized many of the profitable parts of industry and assets to their own advantage. Their fight against a stronger central power should, therefore, also be seen as an attempt to retain their privileged positions and further facilitate their personal enrichment. However, many leaders of weaker agricultural regions actually seem to prefer not to have both the power and the corresponding responsibility.

The 'red directors' of Eastern Ukraine's heavy industry complex, together with those of the agricultural complex, seem to have a strong political influence in Kiev, and they should be expected to remain in opposition or to lobby for slow economic reforms. Little is known about the new business class which still operates in the 'shadow economy', which, according to some, represents up to 50 per cent of the Ukrainian economy. However, there are indications that they support President Kuchma's pragmatic policies and, of course, reforms legalizing their business activities.

Ukraine has inherited Europe's second largest army after Russia, some 700,000 troops, and significant reserves of modern conventional equipment.[5] However, there are serious doubts about Ukraine's ability to defend itself in the event of Russian aggression, because of the Russian domination of the Ukrainian army's officer corps and their close contacts with their counterparts in the Russian army. The ethnic divide, reflecting Ukrainian society, makes it difficult to imagine the army becoming a political player and taking power. If such an attempt took place the army should be expected to split rapidly along ethnic lines. Still, some maintain that the army may step in if Ukraine's territorial integrity were at risk. However, could one expect Russian officers to stop Eastern Ukraine or Crimea from joining Russia? Probably not, and therefore, a non-player role seems more likely for the army. Of course, the army might still shape Ukraine's future by default as awareness of its incapacity could make Ukraine more susceptible to external threats, and more willing to concede to them. Furthermore, the demoralization of the army, which is bound to increase further with the severe down-sizing of the number of troops, could transform it into an uncontrollable institution capable of destabilizing Ukrainian society.

3.5. DEMOCRATIC ELEMENTS

Free and fair elections have taken place, together with a democratic hand-over of power, a test which Russia still has to pass. Apart from this, the Ukraine still has a long way to go before democratic traditions become deeply rooted. Ukrainians say that today the media are the only propagators of democracy, although this is only true for some of them, while most of the others try to guess in advance what will please the President. In addition, most people read only the local press which is usually the subsidized organ of local authority and therefore hardly conducive to the emergence of a democratic civil society. Crimean press is Russian-subsidized in order to ensure a broad sympathetic readership. Television is dominated by Russian state-owned 'Ostankino' which could be expected to use subtle and subliminal messages in the event of trouble between Russia and the Ukraine with a view to reintegrating the latter into the Russian orbit.

3.6. INTERACTIONS BETWEEN PLAYERS AND FACTORS AND TENDENCIES

- *Ukraine's government faces a persistent balancing act*, between Russia and the West, and internally, between its eastern and western populations. Leaning one-sidedly to Russia could reduce the West's (lukewarm) interest and (economic) support and clearly alienate Western Ukraine from Kiev. Leaning too strongly to the West could provoke Russia to pull it back into its orbit and cause strong internal opposition from the Russophone Ukrainians not wanting their 'fraternal' ties to Russia to be cut off.
- *A middle-of-the-road or neutral policy line, as followed by President Kuchma, therefore, seems to be best suited to consolidate the young state*, that is making Ukraine a non-nuclear, non-bloc, regional power with diversified interests, cooperating with all partners

to the detriment of none, with some more closely in the economic field and with others more on matters of security.

- *Economic regeneration is crucial for the consolidation of statehood.* However, Ukraine is in a dilemma since 'shock-therapy' may be internally divisive and for a more managed and regionally balanced economic transition there seems to be a lack of managers. Therefore, one might expect reforms to meet resistance, and the developing entrepreneurial class and workers, who are afraid of losing their jobs, to push for protection from imports. In any case, Ukraine will need to re-establish closer economic ties with Russia and will remain dependent on its energy supplies. Whether this dependence will and can be balanced by Western support is questionable.

- *The prospects are for the Ukraine to maintain its statehood, but having to defer to Russian interests.* This may make neutrality unsustainable. The optimal model for Russian-Ukrainian relations would be the US-Canadian one, or worse, the US-Mexican one. Neither should one exclude the possibility of the country splitting, with Crimea and Eastern Ukraine joining Russia. A failure of economic reforms and growing economic distance between Russia and Ukraine could be conducive to such a development. So, even though Kiev may pursue wise policies, Ukraine's future will still depend on Russia and also on the West.

- *Ukraine, however, will also influence Russia.* 'Without Ukraine, Russia ceases to be an empire, but with Ukraine suborned and then subordinated, Russia automatically becomes an empire' (Z. Brzezinski). Therefore, by supporting Ukraine's independence, the West could also influence Russia's development towards democracy and stability.

Notes

1 Crimea, with its 70 per cent ethnic Russians persistently looking to Russia to support its secessionist ambitions and with 10 per cent

130

Crimean Tartars, is still a case apart and certainly will remain the object of permanent struggle between Russia and Ukraine.

2 The traditional wealth of eastern Ukraine is built on coal, steel and heavy machinery industry whose production facilities are hopelessly outdated.

3 Some say, however, that the eastern regions' aspirations of rejoining Russia are muted by the realization that they would lose political influence as part of a larger Russia and that their industry could be overwhelmed by Russian enterprises.

4 This paper was written in November 1995. At the end of June 1996, a new Constitution was adopted. This clarifies some of the issues regarding the division of power between the President, the government and Parliament, and allows the President to issue decrees on economic issues for the next three years. (It also guarantees private property rights.) Though this is clearly a progress, conflicts seem to continue behind the scenes and may heat up again in the next presidential elections. Therefore, most of what is said here still seems to be valid.

5 Nuclear tactical weapons have already been transferred to Russia, and remaining strategic weapons are now being moved to Russia for decommissioning.

Summary

1. *The break-away from Communism, plunging Russian society head on into a democratic future, has not worked. The historical burden is too heavy.*

- There is more disorientation than orientation, more alienation from everything than adherence to anything, individually as well as collectively.
- Russian society is weak, knowing little self-organization. There are no real trade unions, no strong business associations, no major civil movements. The main preoccupation is the struggle for material survival and people therefore have little time to engage in and develop civil networks.
- A real multi-party system has not yet emerged. There are strong political parties on the left and the right ends of the spectrum, but a black hole in the middle. Since the losers of reforms are likely to outnumber the winners for many more years to come, they cannot be expected to support policies that benefit mostly a small minority. So, there is a potential for large swings in political preferences. Despite the fact that the population at large seems to be waiting for a charismatic leader who can promise to establish law and order, it does not seem prepared to lend support to adventurous and aggressive policies.

2. *It is to be expected that the present type of political regime will consolidate further. This system could be described as 'autocratic presidential' with the Government as an adjunct, an 'emasculated' Parliament as an annex, and a Judiciary that has yet to be developed.*

- However, counter-forces to presidential power have emerged and seem bound to strengthen further. Regional leaders have been democratically elected which makes them less dependent on the President. Russia's new capitalists have acquired not only considerable economic power, but now also control much of the media, rendering them strong political players. Although the President continues to be the main source of legislation, his executive power is strongly reduced by all-embracing corruption preventing proper implementation of legislation.

- There is no effective rule of law and few people seem to have an interest in developing one. For the time being, neither the executive nor the legislative are keen on sharing power with an independent judiciary, and the new capitalists and the bureaucracy seem to be interested in the preservation of the present legal grey-zone, not to speak of the Mafia.

- None of the major players will want too strong a President. The regional leaders do not want too strong a centre, which could eventually cut back on their powers. The capitalists do not want a strong President, since they would stand to lose influence and political backing for the further extension of their economic power. Neither do any of those others (including the Kremlin *kamarilla*) who have somehow profited from the covert privatization of Russia's wealth.

3. Russia's route to capitalism is firmly established.

- However, large parts of the population resent the capitalists. Since a marked improvement of their living standards is not (yet) in sight, but instead a further increase in social inequality, hostility towards the new economic and social system may rise. Still, one should not expect social discontent to develop into violence.

- A market system governed by clear rules and fair economic competition is not yet in sight. The most influential new capitalists now form a silent alliance with the central and regional governments, fuelled by a steady flow of bribe-money and further favours in return. These alliances replace economic competition with monopolies and market structures that are suffocating the creation of social wealth, preventing the population at large from benefiting from reforms. Universally, such alliances have always, sooner or later, cohabited with hidden authoritarian political regimes.

- The prospect that Russia will integrate in the world economy (soon) is unlikely. Submitting Russia to international economic rules and keeping it open to international competition would challenge and reduce the power of the silent alliance. Protectionism will shorten the political agenda for a constructive dialogue with the West, and complicate relations between Russia and the Western world.

4. Russia is striving for control of the post-Soviet space which is perceived as being Russia's legitimate zone of influence. Many of the borders with the newly independent states (as well as between them) are arbitrary and represent potential for conflict. Russia wants to protect the 25 million compatriots living in the 'near abroad'. A protectionist Russia will need the other republics to follow similar economic policies since it is not able to control its borders with them.

- The Russian Army is keen on a new role enhancing its prestige and social status. Becoming the guardian of a sort of *Pax Russica* could serve this purpose.
- Russia's capitalists want access to neighbouring countries' energy and raw material resources as well as to their markets.
- Russia's Orthodox Church considers the post-Soviet space as its spiritual zone of influence, although it tolerates Islam in the south.
- The national mood seems to favour a 'leading role' for Russia in the CIS – a perception propagated by the Presidency.
- Some of the republics look for closer relations with Russia,

especially those with few economic resources or those who, for geographical reasons, are left with little choice other than to accept belonging to the zone of Russian influence. It is expected that Russia will make even greater efforts to pressure and bully (some of) the republics firmly back into its security orbit. Cheap energy supplies would be the main instrument for achieving this goal, not open aggression.

5. *For the time being, Russia will continue to be occupied by internal developments since its revolution is not yet over.*

- New social classes are emerging; social tensions are bound to grow.
- The reforms undertaken, inspired by Western models, will need to be adapted further to Russia's own traditions, particular characteristics *and* to the power balance between the main shaping players.

6. *Based on present tendencies, Russia will not threaten its 'near abroad' nor the rest of the outside world.*

- The population at large wants to live in peace and the younger generations are not enthusiastic about mobilizing for military adventures.
- Neither the regional leaders nor the new capitalists would support aggressive policies as they would rather seek to further consolidate their power.
- The Russian Army is currently in bad shape, and therefore unlikely to undertake any large-scale military operations.

From the five baseline scenarios developed it is concluded that the present 'muddling-through' policies are likely to continue, but will be sustainable only if they are underpinned by increasingly authoritarian features. However, other scenarios should not be excluded.

136

Selected bibliography

- Blackwill, R.D., Braithwaite, R., and Tanake, A., *Engaging Russia*, A Report to the Trilateral Commission, The Triangle Papers: 46, New York, Paris, Tokyo, 1995.
- Cleese, A., Cooper, R., and Sakamoto, Y., eds., *The International System After the Collapse of the East-West Order*, Luxembourg Institute for European and International Studies, Dordrecht, Boston, London, 1994.
- Custine, de, A., *Russische Schatten, Prophetische Briefe aus dem Jahre 1839*, Greno Verlagsgesellschaft GmbH, Nördlingen, 1985.
- Freeland, C., Series of articles from the *Financial Times*, London, 1994–97.
- Gosman, L., *Von den Schrecken der Freiheit, Die Russen – ein Psychogramm*, Rowohlt Berlin Verlag GmbH, Berlin, 1993.
- Internationale Politik, *Restauration der Sowjetunion*, Vol. 11, Bonn, 1995.
- Leonhard, W., *Spiel mit dem Feuer, Rußlands schmerzhafter Weg zur Demokratie*, Gustav Lübbe Verlag, Bergisch Gladbach, 1996.
- Margolina, S., *Rußland: Die nichtzivile Gesellschaft*, Rowohlt Taschenbuch Verlag, Reinbeck bei Hamburg, 1994.
- Odom, W.E., and Dujarric, R., *Commonwealth or Empire? Russia, Central Asia, and the Transcaucasus*, Hudson Institute, Herman Kahn Centre, Indianapolis, Indiana, 1995.
- OECD Economic Surveys, *The Russian Federation 1995*, OECD, Paris, 1995.
- Rahr, A., and Krause, J., *Russia's New Foreign Policy*, Arbeitspapiere zur Internationalen Politik 91, Forschungsinstitut der Deutschen Gesellschaft für Auswärtige Politik e.V., Bonn, 1995.

- Ruge, G., *Weites Land*, Berlin Verlag, Berlin, 1996.
- Sager, D., *Betrogenes Rußland, Jeltzins gescheiterte Demokratie*, C. Bertelsmann, Munich, 1996.
- Schmidt-Häuer, Chr., Series of articles from *Die Zeit*, Hamburg, 1994–96.
- Schmidt-Häuer, Chr., *Rußland in Aufruhr*, R. Pieper GmbH & Co, Munich, 1993.
- *Shaping Actors, Shaping Factors in the former Soviet Union*, unpublished research report containing contributions of researchers from the region, organized by the European Centre for International Security (EUCIS), Starnberg, and commissioned by the Forward Studies Unit of the European Commission.
- Terzani, T., *Gute Nacht Herr Lenin, Reise durch ein zerberstendes Weltreich*, Hoffmann & Campe Verlag, Hamburg, 1993.
- Utkin, A.I., *Russia and the West*, The Graduate Institute of International Studies, Geneva, 1995.
- Yeltsin, B., *The Struggle for Russia*, New York, 1994.

The Forward Studies Unit

The Forward Studies Unit[1] was set up in 1989 as a department of the European Commission reporting direct to the President.

It consists of a multicultural, multidisciplinary team of some 15 staff who are responsible for monitoring the forward march of European integration while identifying structural trends and long-term prospects.

The Commission decision setting the Unit up[2] gave it three tasks:

- to monitor and evaluate European integration to 1992 and beyond;
- to establish permanent relations with national bodies involved in forecasting;
- to work in specific briefs.

The Forward Studies Unit has, to date, produced wide-ranging reports on new issues which, as a result, have frequently found their way into the mainstream of the Commission's work, developing a house style which applies a research method designed to bring out the diversity of Europe (Shaping Factors, Shaping Actors), developing an all-round and/or long-term view which makes it easier to secure consensus above and beyond particular national interests, keeping a watching brief on and an ear open to movement in Europe's societies by setting up links with research and forward studies institutions, and holding regular seminars on specific themes which are attended by prominent figures from the arts, the cultural sphere and universities and representatives of civil society, together with the President or a Member of the European Commission.

The futurological function has gradually developed outside the Unit, within several of the Commission's Directorates-General which are keen to adopt a strategic approach. The Unit serves as a point where all the various future-oriented think-tanks inside the Commission can meet.

For some years now, the need for a forecasting function having grown as the work of the European Union has become wider and more complex, the work programme for the Forward Studies Unit has been updated each year so that it can be reoriented to meet specific needs and towards maximum cooperation with all the Commission departments concerned.

Information about the Unit's current work is put out in the quarterly *Lettre des Carrefours* and on an Internet site.

Notes

1 European Commission, Forward Studies Unit, ARCH-25, Rue de la Loi 200, B-1049 Brussels, tel. +32-2-295-6735, fax. +32-2-295-2305, Internet, http://europa.eu.int
2 Minutes of the 955th meeting of the European Commission, 8 March 1989

Other titles published in this series